Smiles Change Lives: The Smart Orthodontist's
Guide to Growing a Purpose-Driven Practice

© 2020 Dustin S. Burleson, DDS, MBA

ISBN: 978-1-970095-11-1

This book, and the lessons and benefits it can bring to your practice, would have never seen the light of day without the tireless efforts of everyone at both Smiles Change Lives and Burleson Seminars. A very special thank you to Tom Brown and Melanie Johnston at Smiles Change Lives, who put in countless hours of revision and editing. There is no doubt that this publication is a more valuable contribution to the orthodontic profession because of your involvement and input. I'm immensely appreciative and grateful for the opportunity to have worked with you on this book and look forward to the continued progress we all will make in serving more patients in need and changing more lives all over the world.

Also, a very special thank you to Ashley Barnholdt and Marilyn Rodriguez in the Burleson Seminars offices for tolerating and supporting the incalculable number of late-night and early-morning emails, phone calls and chicken-scratch, handwritten notes and edits that we've all made to help make this manuscript as strong as it can possibly be. I'm confident I've still missed something and certain one of my family members will immediately point out a typo or grammatical error. I've never published a book without one and they've never let me forget it. But I'm also confident that this book would have never happened without the tireless commitment to excellence and beautiful design provided by Marilyn and Ashley. Thank you for helping us change the world one smile at a time!

And to the reader, I thank you for your investment of time, energy and money in helping make your world and ours a better place for those who can benefit most from our skills and expertise as orthodontists. I hope this book serves as a springboard and statement of gratitude for your continued generosity and abundant worldview.

To your continued success,

Dustin S. Burleson, DDS, MBA

President, Burleson Seminars
Founder, Burleson Orthodontics & Pediatric Dentistry
Director, The Leo H. Rheam Foundation for Cleft & Craniofacial Orthodontics
Adjunct Assistant Clinical Professor, UMKC School of Dentistry, Department of Orthodontics and Dentofacial Orthopedics
Attending Orthodontist, The Children's Mercy Hospital, Kansas City, Missouri

TABLE OF CONTENTS

FOREWORD

When I started Smiles Change Lives in 1997 with my mother, Virginia Brown, there were no other access to care programs helping families afford braces for their children. Wanting to make a difference, we decided that we would help fill that void by starting a foundation to help children in the Kansas City area get braces. In a matter of years, the program expanded to multiple states. We quickly decided we needed to transition to a public charity we called the Virginia Brown Community Orthodontic Partnership, which is now known as Smiles Change Lives.

As we started in Kansas City, early on we worked closely with the University of Missouri-Kansas City Dental School where we met Dr. Dustin Burleson, who was a student there at the time. Dustin has remained involved with our organization over the years, and he has continued to champion our organization not only through the children he has treated but through his efforts to spread the word about our program to other orthodontists. This book is a collaboration between us, which provides the unique opportunity to learn about Smiles Change Lives from both my viewpoint, as founder, CEO and Board President, as well as Dustin's, a partnering orthodontist.

"What is Smiles Change Lives and why should I participate?" are the two most commonly asked questions by orthodontists approached to join our program. Over the course of this book, Dustin and I will share a detailed explanation of Smiles Change Lives and how it operates, as well as provide the answer to why Dustin chose to participate and why we believe that every orthodontist should participate too.

Smiles Change Lives' model is unique in that it is truly a partnership between all the parties involved- the orthodontists and their staff, the family of the child, and our industry partners. Smiles Change Lives' brings all these things together. To date, over 14,000 children have received braces through our program. This is thanks to the work, dedication and support of everyone who has been associated with Smiles Change Lives over the years including orthodontists, families, business partners, referring dentists, board members, employees and volunteers among others.

Our orthodontists participate for many reasons as will be described in the book, but the biggest and most important benefit of working with Smiles Change Lives is knowing that a life has been changed forever - not only of the child treated but the parents, family and all the people who are associated with them. This is a piece of immortality that few people ever get to experience.

I invite you to join us. I can assure you that by doing so, you will achieve positive results.

Thomas C. Brown

Smiles Change Lives, CEO and Board President

"WE CAN CHANGE THE WORLD
AND MAKE IT A BETTER PLACE.
IT IS IN YOUR HANDS TO
MAKE A DIFFERENCE."

— NELSON MANDELA

INTRODUCTION

"Incredible things in the business world are never made by a single person, but by a team." – Steve Jobs

If you are looking to grow your practice, you've found the right book. After all, if you don't continuously grow, you will become stagnant, lose out to the competition, and never reach the level of success that you've always dreamed of. Every entrepreneur has been right where you are. But as you know, entrepreneurs are the most-misunderstood, under-appreciated and often most-disrespected people on the planet. The good news is that with the authors of this book, you are in good company. Scratch that, you are in excellent company.

We have walked countless miles in your shoes. We have had that same intense longing to grow our practice, combined with wanting to make a meaningful difference in the world. Now it's time for you to take that leap in the right direction toward achieving both of those things. Being experts in the industry, we know how you can take your practice to the next level, what it entails, and why you should do it. By the time you're finished here, you will want to get involved in supporting your community while reaping the magnificent rewards of doing so.

We want to challenge you to not only grow your business but also to do it in a unique way. We will give you the platform to do good, which will make you feel good. You may have considered the idea of doing pro bono work before, and regardless of how you feel about it, we want you to set those thoughts aside. The program we are going to share with you is so different that you won't even want to compare the two ideas. Essentially, the system we are going to share with you on these pages starts with the pro bono foundation, but it turns it into something so much more. It makes the idea of pro bono work seem undeniably attractive. Plus, it comes with some serious benefits to your practice.

Sit back, relax, and learn how your orthodontic practice can soar to the top of your industry simply by teaming up with Smiles Change Lives (SCL).

The SCL Story

Before we get into the nuts and bolts of how being a part of SCL can help grow your business, it's important that you have an idea of what the program is all about. SCL isn't something that just sprung up overnight. Like most success stories, the foundation for it began long before anyone saw the fruits of its labor. In order to understand the impact that SCL has on people and where the passion for the program came from, we need to go back to the beginning. It all started with something we are all familiar with: someone who was in desperate need of braces.

Picture living in Chicago during the Great Depression and being in serious need of braces to straighten your teeth. Now imagine that your sister also needs braces and your parents know they can only afford to get one child the treatment they need. Now imagine that you are not the one who gets picked to have the braces. Your sister is the one who gets to have the treatment, leaving you to continue through your school years having teeth that bring about some awful bouts of teasing.

That's exactly what happened to a young lady by the name of Virginia Brown, who happens to be Tom Brown's mother. Having spent her adolescent years being terribly teased because she was in such desperate need of braces, she developed a deep sense of compassion for those who shared such an experience. Finally, able to get the corrective treatment she needed in her early 20s, it set her on a path to help make a difference for others.

Virginia knew the pain and turmoil of having crooked teeth. She knew how awful it made her feel and how it stole her confidence and sense of self-esteem. Having endured so much ridicule and pain, she vowed to do something to help other children in need of braces who come from families that may not be able to afford it.

That set her on a mission – and as you know a woman on a mission is not someone to reckon with. As the years went on, she never lost sight of her passion to help others in need of braces, those who may not have the financial means to pay for them.

That's where the story of SCL, starts but that is only the beginning. The beginning of something extraordinary that has helped many people, including the patients who have undergone treatment and the orthodontists who have provided it to them.

In the Beginning

The beginning of SCL was gathered in the heart of one person, and it blossomed from there into something that has touched thousands of people around the nation. In 1983, Virginia Brown and her late husband created the Virginia and Maurice Brown Foundation. The foundation was donor-advised, where funds were raised and used to help children who needed oral surgery, particularly that of cleft lip and palate. Their mission made a grand difference for those who suffered from these conditions and enabled them to live normal and successful lives. These individuals felt good about themselves and obtained the confidence to chase their dreams and live out their passions.

When Virginia's husband died, she teamed up with her son Tom, and co-founder Dr. Kelly Toombs – together they put the wheels in motion to take the foundation and develop it further. They met with numerous experts to discuss the possible ways to go about offering medical care to children. At the time, there were no programs in the country that provided kids with the necessary orthodontic care they were in desperate need of.

That was how the partnership was formed, and it then evolved into SCL.

SCL fills a need that was previously being unmet. It began working with orthodontists around the country to provide the free care needed, and there are tens of thousands of patients who have completed treatment satisfactorily. Those who complete the program are extremely grateful for having been able to be a part of it. And in doing so, they essentially shout it out from the rooftops.

That's part of the beauty of what keeps this program working so well. Every happy family that participates in the program goes on to sing the praises of the orthodontist who provided the treatment and the program, SCL, that made it possible.

As an orthodontist, how much would you need to spend to advertise, to hear the good word on the streets? A lot. But when you work with SCL, all you are doing is giving your time. What you get back is far more than what you put in. The program offers a positive experience for everyone involved, one that can help your business grow in a unique way.

How it Works

As an orthodontist, you would probably like to support your community by helping children in need of treatment. The problem is - you don't actually know who is deserving, who qualifies financially, who would practice good oral hygiene habits to ensure their teeth remain healthy, who would be compliant, and so on. There are so many decisions to be made about supporting others in need that orthodontists often throw in the towel, in the opposite direction, and don't support their community at all.

One of the most important aspects to SCL is that we take the guesswork out of helping those in need. We handle the entire screening process and select the candidates that we feel meet the qualifications.

Once someone is selected by our program and matched with an orthodontist, it is still the choice of the practice owner whether they want to provide the pro bono treatment to the candidate. We simply match you up with vetted candidates.

Orthodontists around the country appreciate this process, because it's fair, it's simple, and it saves them a lot of time. They don't have to feel bad telling someone in their office that they can't provide complimentary treatment. They never have to say "no" or ask tough

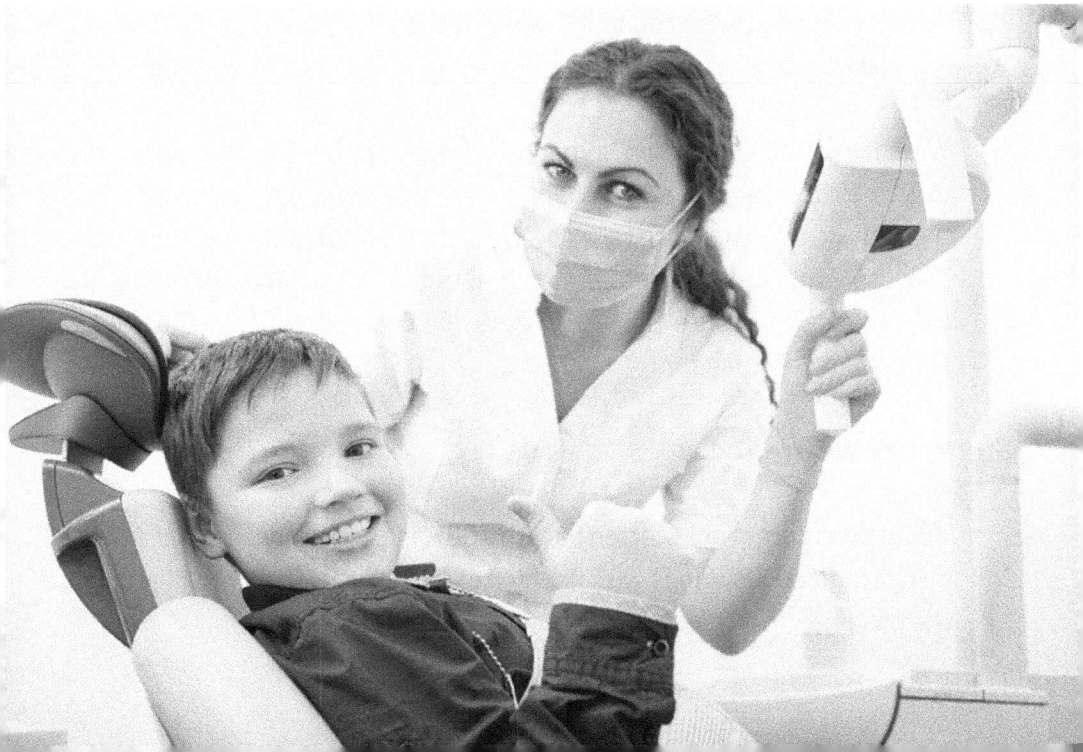

questions. Instead, they will only be matched with those who have been through our screening process and have been selected as a good-treatment candidate.

A challenge that many orthodontists have had with providing pro bono treatment is that the people often do not comply with instructions. That can be extremely frustrating for someone who has invested their time, effort, and appliances, only to see the person not hold up their end of the agreement. At SCL, we tackle that problem for you. We have a different take on supporting the community than many other people do.

We believe in giving a hand up, rather than a hand out. And that has made all the difference.

When someone who isn't financially well off works hard to come up with $650 for their child to have treatment, you better believe you will have a compliant patient on your hands. The parent is invested, and as such, they will ensure that their child listens to your recommendations, follows your treatment guidelines, and is a good patient. We also only consider patients who have good oral hygiene and an established dental home, where a licensed dentist has verified that any areas of tooth decay have been restored prior to recommending orthodontic treatment.

We have found that when someone comes through the SCL program, they are also far more compliant than those who pay thousands for their braces. Orthodontists who are a part of our network love that because compliant patients are the best kind to have. We partner with the families to ensure their child gets the orthodontic care they need but cannot fully pay for.

Where We Are Today

Our little program got started back in 1997 and has grown exponentially, doing tremendous things with the help of generous orthodontists around the country.

There are well over 14,000 children who have successfully completed orthodontic treatment through the SCL program. We have over 750 orthodontists in our network who provide treatment to those we have screened and selected. As a nonprofit organization whose mission is to provide access to orthodontic care for children whose families can't afford the full cost of treatment, we are thrilled with how far we have come and all that we have done. The SCL program has provided $70,000,000 worth of orthodontic care to patients to date.

Growing Your Practice

At this point, you have a good idea of where the SCL program came from, what the mission is, and how it works. But you might be wondering, how can SCL possibly help to tremendously grow my practice if I am providing free orthodontic care? Pro bono work is wonderful, but, by definition, it means "without pay." So, I would not really be getting any kind of financial benefit for doing this work, right?

That's where you would be wrong. Dead wrong.

What you will learn in the pages of this book is just how effectively you can grow your practice in a unique way by joining our network of board-certified orthodontists who provide pro bono care. We have not only created a way to carry out Virginia's mission of helping families in need to get their children the braces they need, but the by-product of the program is what it gives back to the orthodontists who participate.

Imagine providing carefully selected children with treatment to straighten their teeth for free. But there's a caveat, in that we provide the hardware, retainers, etc. And it doesn't stop there. We also take care of the public relations that will get you noticed when you do provide those pro bono services. We handle public relations in your local area, which can be used to spread the message on social media, television, newspapers, and more. Plus, you will have additional people spreading the good word about how you are involved in supporting your community.

By providing pro bono care, you are supporting your community in a meaningful way and helping kids in an incredible way that will benefit them for the rest of their lives. Everyone loves a provider who not only helps them financially but also who gives their child a confident smile for life. The hand up that is being provided will go a long way toward helping your business to get publicity, a great reputation, referrals, and much more.

Every orthodontist in our network has been established as someone who graciously supports their community members. They receive many referrals, goodwill, and the amazing feeling that comes with doing something fantastic for someone. Especially because you provide this service to children in need. That is, quite literally, life-changing!

Those in the orthodontic field know just how important it is to have straight teeth and a smile that a person loves when they look in the mirror. A great smile can give people confidence, raise their self-esteem

and sense of self-value, and it can make drastic changes in their life. Those with straight teeth and a nice smile will be more likely to feel comfortable giving a presentation in front of their class, to ask someone to the prom, and to do better in college and job interviews. Not being held back by crooked teeth means the sky is the limit and for many people our program is not just a hand up, it's a huge boost up.

The orthodontists we work with cover the entire United States and Canada. Virginia always believed that a child being able to get the braces they need should not be a luxury; every child deserves to feel good about their smile! We continue with that motto and focus.

So many entrepreneurs dream of changing lives and supporting others in a meaningful way. Through our organization, orthodontists do this on a regular basis, and they are recognized for it from sea to shining sea.

In the following chapters, we are going to share with you how you can grow your orthodontic practice in unique ways with SCL being one of them. We'll take an in-depth look at everything from marketing and public relations to attracting the best employees and building your legacy. Many of the ideas you hear may seem unconventional or make you raise your eyebrows. Good! That's exactly what we want. When it comes to becoming a major success in your field, you have two options: Go big or go home. It's some hard truth, but that's the way it is. This is one field where you cannot be vanilla. We will be the first to tell you that vanilla only works with ice cream. Being vanilla, or boring and playing it safe, will never ever take you to the big leagues. Your practice will remain right where it is unless you go big.

You can benefit from our vast array of experience in this field. As one of the authors of this book, I give to you my wealth of experience in how to create a major connection to your community. If you want to grow your practice, having strong ties to your community is a highly effective way to go about doing so. On the other end, you are getting advice in this book from the highest-paid orthodontic consultant on the planet.

We want your practice to grow and succeed beyond your wildest dreams. We know you want that as well. But we also know that, like most other orthodontists, you aren't quite sure how to go about making that happen. Let us be clear on something that you must grasp if are to thrive. You can be the best orthodontist on earth planet, but if you fail to go big, think unique, and reach beyond your comfort zone, then you will end up just being, well, vanilla.

It is inherently important that you realize you must be willing to work "on" your practice and not just "in" your practice. By considering the unique ways to grow your business that we are suggesting throughout this book, you will be working on your business in a major way. We will offer ideas, tips, and tools that will help you understand more about how to attract highly desirable patients, how to get people to talk about how amazing your practice is, and what you need to do to get a constant stream of referrals.

We know what it takes, because we've done it, and then some. We've had our own failures along the way, we've conquered them, learned from them, and have come out stronger and far more successful as a result. Not only do we want to share what we know will help grow your business, but also shout it from the mountaintops.

We want you to succeed in a major way, and we are going to show you how to do it in unique ways. Read on with an open mind and a sense of eagerness, because this is the first step in your journey to take your practice to the next level.

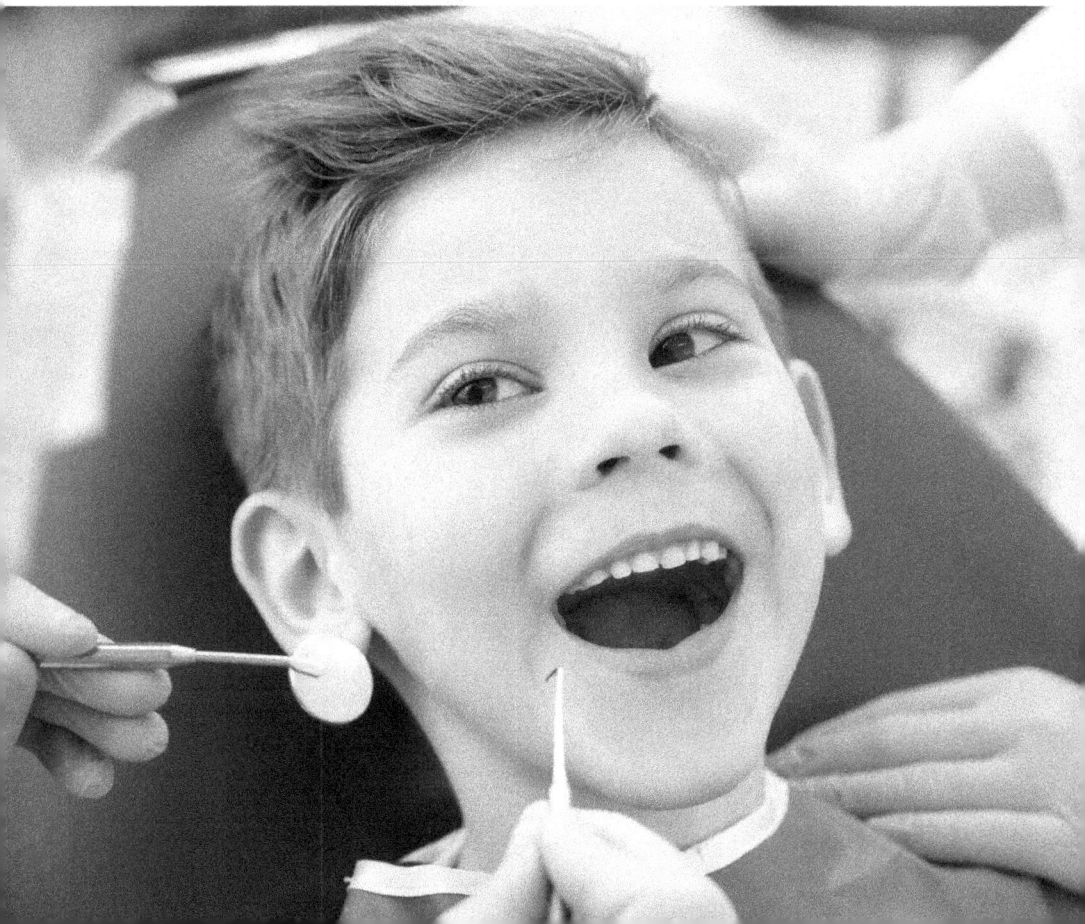

CHAPTER 1

MEET YOUR NEW MARKETING DEPARTMENT

"The highest use of capital is not to make more money but to make money to do more for the betterment of life."
– Henry Ford

Philanthropy, by definition, is the desire to promote the welfare of others. It's something that is done by the generous donations of money to causes. It's probably the last thing you would ever think of as a marketing tool, but I'm here to tell you otherwise. I know for a fact that it's a highly effective marketing strategy and that it can do wonders for your practice.

I've used the power of philanthropy in my practice for many years, have been a big proponent of singing the praises of it to others and will continue to use it as the amazing resource that it is. For many dentists and orthodontists, however, philanthropy is largely an untapped resource and one that most have never taken the time to fully consider. In all honesty, this has been to their loss, but once you read on, it won't be to yours.

Unique Approaches

When you picked up this book, you knew that you were going to be introduced to a unique approach to growing your practice. Many people have an aversion to being unique. They are afraid to take a different path or do their own thing. They spend more time looking at what their competition is doing than looking at what they could be doing. If you want your practice to be a huge success you must absolutely embrace the idea that being unique is a good thing. You can't be afraid to stand out or receive attention from your peers.

Let me share a little about why I say that. I didn't get to where I am today because I played it safe and cared deeply about what my competition thinks of me. Sure, it's nice if people like me, but not at the expense of keeping my practice from growing. I want to stand out, get noticed, and take a completely different approach. My number one goal is not to be the most- loved orthodontist amongst my peers.

I have strategically laughed at what others take too seriously, and I have embraced the things they won't do. This is especially true from outside of our industry and with other professions. What others take seriously, I often see as foolish, such as peer status, networking and awards. What others take as foolish or leave up to chance, well, those are the things I take dead seriously.

Unique marketing, like encouraging the kids who are treated through SCL to tell their friends and family about my practice, is just one example of something which we heavily focus on that others do not – it's a major reason why we enjoy tremendous success.

Most people search out the wrong rewards from philanthropy. They want to be recognized, and they want to feel good. This is an inherently limiting way to see the world. It makes the charitable act all about you. I see the world more like Henry Ford, leveraging philanthropy to generate more wealth so that everyone thrives. I don't see money as an evil thing. Money won't make you happy, but it won't make you unhappy either. If my practices fail to thrive, how many kids could I help through Smiles Change Lives each year? Only by thriving can my charitable work help more people. I'm not shy about sharing that message. Now, before there are grumbles in the audience, let me explain my position on that.

Feeling Good Goes Both Ways

We all know that doing philanthropy work is a good thing, right? I think that's something we can all agree on. You are helping others, which in turn helps society. But you get something in return, and you shouldn't feel bad about it. I'm paraphrasing, but Edward Kramer explained, "The hole you give through is the hole you receive through."

Research shows that when we help others, we become happier ourselves. Those who receive the help become happier too. It's a full circle of happiness and feel-good chemicals that are released in our brains, and it improves our quality of life. Most people don't want to think about what they get in return, because they have been led to believe that philanthropy is just all about helping the other person.

What's wrong with enjoying and embracing the good benefits you get in return? Not a damned thing, if you ask me. In fact, I think you should learn to love it and do more of it for what you get in return. I know, it's not the popular stance, but I warned you that I'm not about chasing after the popular route that others may take. I see something that is good for us, bringing about multiple benefits, and I think we should choose to make it a routine part of our life.

My grandfather was a Pennsylvania State Trooper. I grew up watching John Wayne movies with him. There was always something about the strong yet calm character and presence in both my grandfather and John Wayne that captivated me. In Scott Eyman's biography of Wayne, he explores the more complex character and persona we see on film versus the conservative movie icon we think we all know.

Wayne said, "Tomorrow is the most important thing in life. Comes into us at midnight very clean. It's perfect when it arrives and it puts itself in our hands. It hopes we've learned something from yesterday." He was making a personal admission of past failures and hopes for his own future, not just playing some character on the big screen.

In the early days of my practice, I didn't understand the power of philanthropy. I missed the mark on how abundant my worldview needed

IMAGINE WHAT
THE WORLD WOULD BE
LIKE IF EVERYONE GAVE
MORE SIMPLY BECAUSE
THEY LOVED WHAT THEY
GOT IN RETURN.

to be and how generously I gave to those in need. Luckily, like Wayne, I learned something from my yesterdays. As a result, my tomorrows were and continue to be much more successful and abundant, where everyone around me thrives.

Think about going to the gym. When you engage in regular exercise, you feel good and you get health benefits in return. You don't feel ashamed or try to downplay it and act as though you merely did it for the sake of exercise itself. That's how I used to think about philanthrophy. I occasionally did good by helping patients who couldn't afford treatment because I thought it was the right thing to do. But I only did this sporadically. It wasn't an integral part of my practice like it is today.

When I stopped being shy and fully embraced what I got in return, my practice tripled in size. Then it tripled again in less than 18 months. Learn from my yesterdays. Give generously and embrace what you get in return. It's a good thing. It will help strengthen the reasons why you give in the first place and it gets more people interested in giving too.

Imagine what the world would be like if everyone gave more simply because they love what they get in return. Everyone would be happier as a result. Those who are receiving would be happier, those who are giving would be happier, and the cycle would continue.

Any way you look at it, giving is good for multiple reasons. You know it makes you a happier person, which is a great thing, but now let's look at how it can help your practice to grow.

Your New Marketing Department

As an orthodontist, there's no doubt you've been asked to treat someone in your community for free. Perhaps a family from your church or synagogue needs assistance or someone from a community center or school association has sought out your help for a child or an entire family that needs help. You were trained in school to help others and, if you're like me, you've taken on these cases and provided pro-bono services whenever requested.

The problem with many pro-bono cases, unfortunately, is poor compliance. Hygiene and appointment continuity are typically far worse with these patients that you treat for free. This isn't my "gut reaction" either. The data from our own practices and from our coaching clients suggests that compliance is worse with any case where there isn't "skin in the game."

This is the problem Smiles Change Lives has solved for hundreds of orthodontists and thousands of deserving children. Because the organization asks the parents to make an investment in the smile of their child (at the time of this writing the total investment for parents is $650), we see significantly better compliance and outcomes.

I've taught for years at Burleson Seminars that Smiles Change Lives takes all the headaches out of treating pro-bono cases. As an orthodontist, I simply get to transform smiles and SCL takes care of the rest. Patients are happy, parents are happy and (best of all) they show up, take great care of their teeth and they are extremely appreciative for the work we do. It's a win-win-win.

Years ago, I only took one or two Smiles Change Lives patients per year. I'll talk more about "the capacity myth" in chapter five, but for now, let's fast forward to present day. At the time of this writing, our office accepts nearly every patient Smiles Change Lives can send our way. We've treated hundreds of patients, and we hope they keep sending more and more. Why?

Because these kids aren't poor. They are low income. Poor kids have a social safety net. They have Medicaid or other federal or state assistance. These kids do not. Often, they are immigrants and their parents work two or three jobs just to make ends meet. A $650 investment is a big deal for these families, and they also know they are receiving the gift of a lifetime of smiles and confidence for their child, so they are more than appreciative for what we've done. We're not shy about asking them to send their friends and family our way.

These kids sit in school next to your kids. These parents work in buildings where your patients and their parents work. They are not "Medicaid" patients and they are not the type of people who want a handout. As such, they are more than happy to spread the word about your practice and the good you do in your community. They want to be accepted and treated just like everyone else, and we help make that happen. Not just by providing them with treatment, but by treating them just the same as we treat everyone else.

You'll love working with Smiles Change Lives because they have a tested and proven screening (i.e., vetting) process in place to help identify not only qualified but also motivated candidates for orthodontic treatment. The team at Smiles Change Lives handles all of the case acceptance and management issues, so that in the rare situation when a problem arises, you and your office don't have to take time out of your schedule to deal with and handle these requests.

Also, working with Smiles Change Lives means never having to say "no." The doctor can always be the "hero" and send as many people as possible to Smiles Change Lives, knowing that the organization will be the one to say "no" to patients who are not qualified, not committed or, in their experience, won't be a great fit for orthodontic treatment in the program. In speaking with many of the doctors in the program and those who are considering joining and working with Smiles Change Lives, this is one of the biggest selling points. Helping kids and families in need is easy with Smiles Change Lives. They do all the heavy lifting.

Sincere Referrals

When you think about your marketing department, you most likely picture a person or group of people who work together to get your name out there.

They are considered your marketing team, and they do what you pay them to do. However, there are some things that they won't be able to do. Marketing efforts, as you and I know, can only go so far. I've also worked with enough orthodontists around the world providing consulting that I know many don't pay a bit of attention to their marketing. They spend money, sure, but they don't manage it in order to see what's effective or not. They don't know what they are getting out of it, and they usually have no idea if their marketing is bringing them new referrals and, if so, how many.

That's what's different about the patients I refer to as my marketing department. I essentially pay them in treatment and they, in turn, bring me lots of referrals. Think about it for a moment. You pay your marketing person

or department to do what? To focus on your brand, get you noticed, and on and on. But when it comes right down to the bare bones of it, what are you really paying them for? You are paying them to bring you referrals.

Your practice, if you want it to become wildly successful, relies upon a steady stream of referrals. You need new patients like plants need sunlight. If you want to exist, grow and thrive, it's a must. What I've learned over the years is that philanthropy work with the Smiles Changes

---

As I've said many times, it's truly a win-win-win situation.
It's brilliant, and one that would be difficult to beat. Everyone loves a doctor who provides pro-bono treatment to someone in need who can't afford to pay for it all. You come out way ahead with the benefits you receive, the child is given a life-changing opportunity, and everyone goes home as happy as can be.

Lives program brings in referrals, and a lot of them. Remember what I said about how when you give you are going to get a lot back in return. Along with feeling good and becoming a happier person, you are going to get a steady stream of referrals, too. And guess what? That will also add to the good feelings and being happier. When you see referral after referral coming to your office, it can't help but to put a smile on your face. Smiles really do change lives, a lot of them.

We lovingly refer to our hundreds of active Smiles Change Lives patients as our marketing department because they are. These patients are the first to bring friends and family to our patient appreciation events. They are the first to sign up for my latest book or report, and they share them with their friends, family and co-workers. Not only are Smiles Change Lives patients great to work with, but they have referred hundreds of new patients to my practices that are cash-paying or have dental insurance.

It's not uncommon for Smiles Change Lives families to come back years later and pay for one of the next kid's treatment. They were so appreciative that we helped them when times were tough financially that when they got back on their feet, they were more than happy to pay our full fee for orthodontic treatment for the next kid in the family.

Every child I provide treatment to through the Smiles Change Lives program, becomes a walking and talking billboard for my practice. Their parents become some of my biggest cheerleaders. I have an army of current and former patients who are part of my marketing team. That marketing team also includes their parents, aunts, uncles, grandparents, and anyone else who knows the story of how they got their beautiful smile. Once people hear the story of an orthodontist who provided the child with treatment for free, they can't help but to love what you did and share that with others.

It's a virtually unstoppable marketing team that you are building when you provide treatment to the kids in the program. Not only are they and their families going to tell everyone, but Smiles Change Lives is wonderful with their public relations abilities. They reach out on your behalf and get the information out there about your efforts. You are not tooting your own horn, everyone else is doing it for you, which makes it much more valuable. That's simply unmatched in terms of marketing and exposure and it's something that will have a drastic impact on your practice. Your practice will be seen in a new light, have plenty of referrals, everyone will be feeling happy from helping others, and all will be well.

I have a firm belief that a creative mindset, versus a competitive one, allows you to see that you can be paid based on the results you generate and not just the time you clock in and out. The results I'm generating when I work with the Smiles Changes Lives patients, for example, are happy families who have a child who will become more confident and will likely have a better quality of life from their treatment. Those are results I'd love to be paid for, rather than just how many hours a week I put into the office. I want to be known for and paid for the life-changing treatments that I provide and the outcomes that have an impact on people.

Patient Treatment

Because my practices are known for doing a lot of gifting, notes, phone calls, and personalized follow-up, I'm often asked if we put our Smiles Change Lives patients through the same experience as our full-fee patients. The answer is yes, absolutely. We send birthday cards and small gifts to our patients and that includes our Smiles patients. We send new patients "wow" boxes when they get their braces on. These kits include T-shirts, electric toothbrushes, and other fun gifts and we absolutely send them to our Smiles Change Lives patients as well.

If you set the expectation that Smiles Change Lives patients are treated like every other patient in your practice, you'll see these patients refer more patients to you than you ever imagined possible.

Think back to the stigma of food stamps from many decades ago. When I was a kid, I remember the "Food Stamp Line" at the grocery store. You had to go stand in line in a separate area, away from everyone else who was paying cash. It was embarrassing and stigmatizing. Do you want to create that kind of experience for your Smiles Change Lives patients? Absolutely not. Treat them like the valuable, unique, amazing patients that they are. Treat them with love and respect. Crawl through broken glass for them in how you provide customer service and they can quite literally transform the landscape of your practice through referrals.

Not only do these patients deserve the same treatment you provide to everyone else, but how your team treats them speaks volumes about your office. If you treat them as a special case and don't give them the same treatment that your paying patients get, then that is the word that will be on the street. Treat them with the same respect, dignity, and consideration, and it shows what a class act your team is. The message that your office will be sending is that you don't care who a patient is or how much money they have; you love all of your patients and treat them all equally.

Believe me when I say that people will notice how you treat them. We have all seen those stories in the news about a waitress or other service person who receives a large, over-the-top unexpected tip for doing their job. That person can't wait to share their good fortune with others, and it's a good reminder for us all that there are still a lot of good people in the world.

Some patients coming to your office under the SCL program may expect to get treatment that isn't the same as what your regularly paying patients receive. Imagine how blown away they will be when they find out that is not the case at all! You can be assured that they will be appreciative of your kindness and will become your biggest cheerleader.

Every patient at our practices is treated as an equal, regardless of their payment source, ability to pay, or how they came to us. Our mission is to turn out beautiful smiles for everyone that we provide treatment to. In order to do that, we are committed to providing an amazing experience that will make people feel valued and make them want to tell others about our office. If we do that, we have succeeded and everything else will fall into place.

Marketing Smarter

I've worked with doctors around the world, helping them identify what's missing in their practices. I'm brutally honest in telling them where they are going wrong, what they need to do in order to make improvements and exactly what it will take to reach the level of success they want. Marketing is one area where most orthodontists fail miserably.

Most offices are spending some money on marketing but that's about all their marketing efforts are doing. They usually have no idea where their referrals are coming from and if their marketing efforts are paying off. They usually don't know what works, what doesn't, and they are rarely ever engaging in anything unique. Marketing is one of the most poorly understood areas of just about any orthodontic practice. It's a tool that is underutilized and overpaid for. Having a big marketing budget doesn't mean a whole lot. You can throw money in a lot of directions, but that doesn't mean it will effectively grow your practice and it's not guaranteed to bring you raving fans of your office.

If you want to grow your practice, you must make an important decision to become a smarter marketer. This means taking a new approach, and in this book, we explain in detail why philanthropy is a great way to do this. When you use philanthropy to get more referrals, you will be marketing smarter, and it's going to reap many rewards. And here's the good thing: those rewards will not just be there for you, although they will be in abundance for your office, they will also be there for the patients, their families, and for the community.

There's just no better way to put it. When you give through philanthropy, you get back so much more.

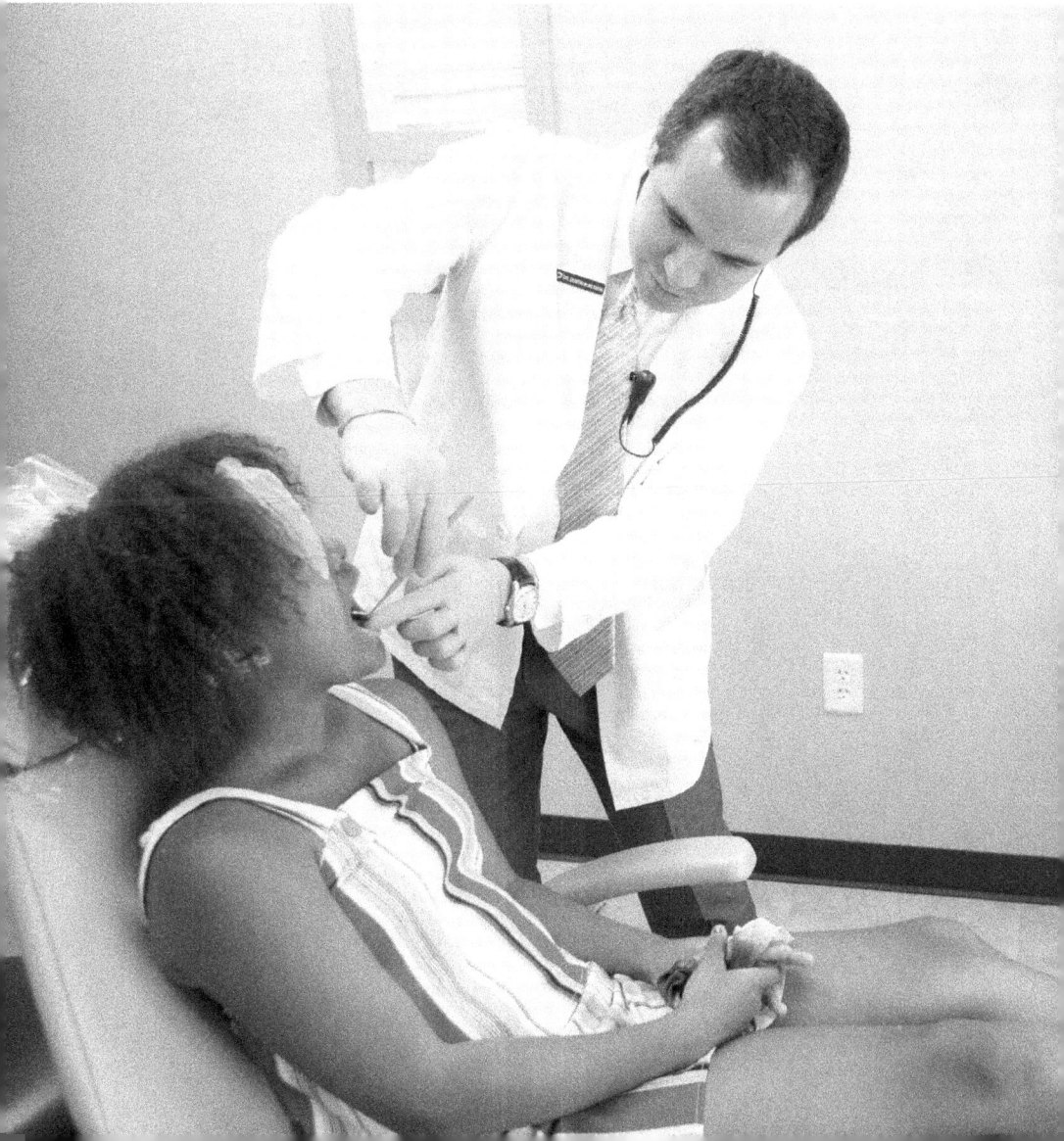

CHAPTER 2:

PR THE SMART WAY

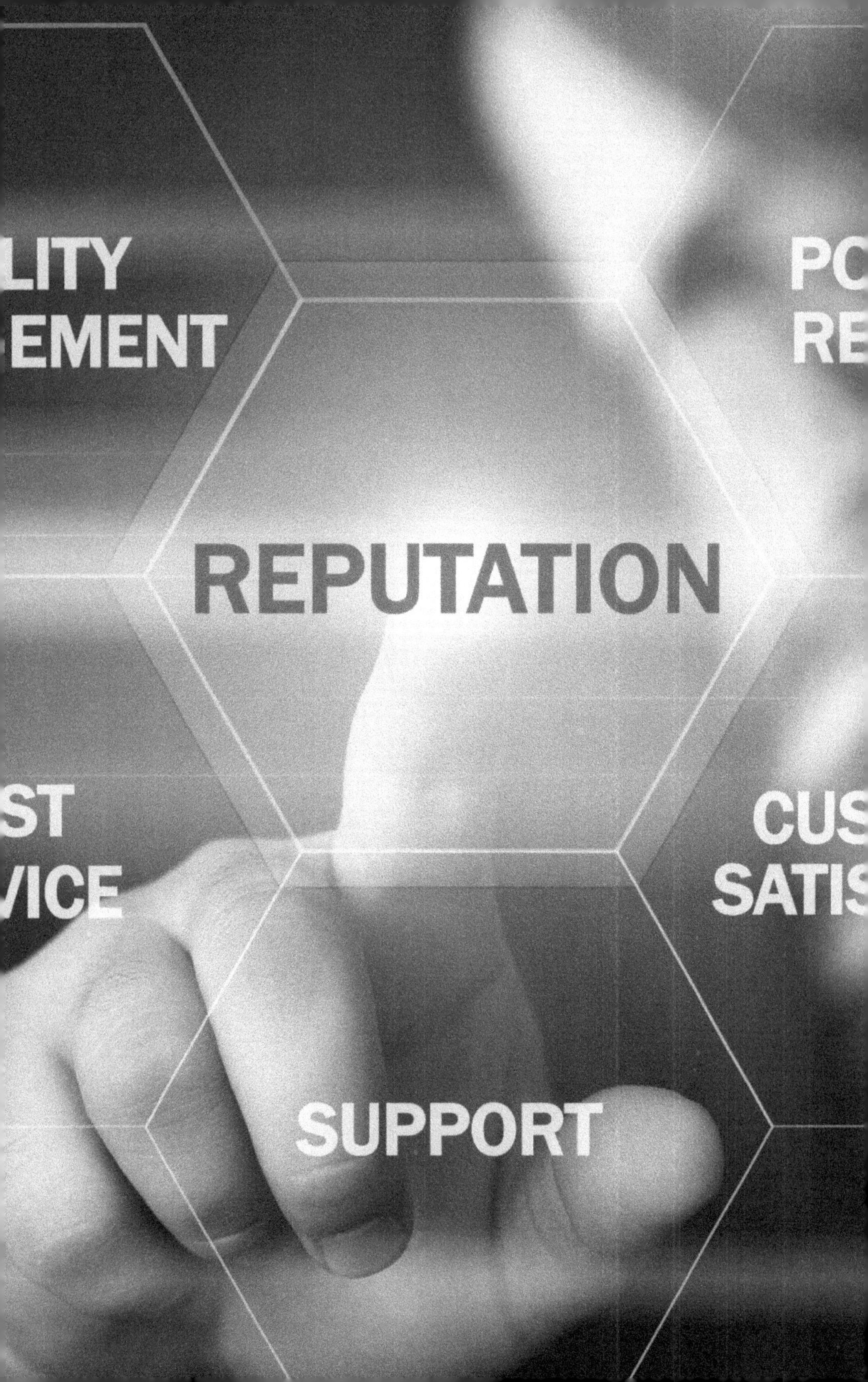
LITY
EMENT
REPUTATION
ST
VICE
SUPPORT

*"Publicity is absolutely critical. A good PR story
is infinitely more effective
than a front page ad." – Richard Branson*

If you are not taking advantage of all that publicity has to offer your practice, then you are leaving a lot behind. I can't express enough how much you are missing out on. Publicity is the greatest tool, or rather gift, that any business can acquire. The more you learn about it, the more you will want to leverage the power of it in order to grow your business and strengthen your position in the community.

In all my years of working with other orthodontists through my consulting and seminars, if I had to choose the biggest mistake that they make, not leveraging the power of publicity would have to rank at the top. It has to be one of the most important things a business can have but it's often the most overlooked. If you are not taking advantage of publicity, then you are making a big mistake. But don't worry, after you read this you will have a great idea why it's so important and you will be ready to make it a big part of your professional life.

Defining Publicity

Not long ago, there was a story in the news about a toddler who had gotten ahold of money that the parents were saving up to purchase sports tickets. They had been saving the money in the home and when they went to get the $1,000 it was gone. Come to find out, their toddler had some fun with it, putting it through the shredder. The family, who is not well off, was distraught and posted about it on social media. That post went viral, with all of their friends and family sharing it.

Dr. Pepper, the soda company, saw the mishap and stepped up. They chose to replace the $1,000 so these parents could buy the concert tickets. Simple act, right? Yes, but also very clever. Dr. Pepper leveraged the power of publicity in a way that very few companies do. It was nothing short of genius.

Why was it a genius act of publicity by Dr. Pepper? Because their story of generosity hit news outlets from coast to coast, was shared over and over online, and was seen by millions of people. You can't buy that kind of publicity. They put out $1,000 to help a family in need and in turn they got back a mountain of great publicity. That act of kindness elevated the company in many people's eyes. As little of an act as it was, at least to most people, it meant the world to that family. And most families can relate to the loss and then someone stepping up to provide the help they needed.

Whatever traditional advertising Dr. Pepper could have purchased for that same amount of money pales in comparison to the enormous return they received from a very small cash investment.

Everyone knows that you are going to make yourself look good. They trust the newspapers and television stations to not be as biased and to bring you third party opinions and experiences. The masses trust publicity far more than they ever trust any type of advertising that you can do.

Publicity Rules

In my own practice, I have used publicity a lot. It's a tool that I strongly believe in and try to encourage other orthodontists to use as often as possible. Once you give it a try and see what it can do for you, then you will become another cheerleader for publicity, too. It's critical that

WHAT SOMEONE ELSE SAYS ABOUT YOUR PRACTICE IS GOING TO BE FAR MORE BENEFICIAL THAN ANYTHING YOU CAN SAY YOURSELF.

every orthodontist on the planet understand publicity, how to get it, and why it's so important in helping to grow their business.

Many doctors ask how I'm able to get on the radio and television and in the news so consistently over many years. Here's the secret: what other people say about you is far more powerful than anything you say about yourself.

You can say you care about your community all you want, but it may fall on deaf ears.Let people in the community who have benefited from your help, or know someone who has, tell others about you. It's more powerful when someone else says something good about you. Very powerful indeed.

Try calling every television newsroom and asking to speak with the producer because you want to talk on their program about orthodontics. I hope you're prepared to hear the sound of telephone after telephone hanging up in your ear. Ask me how I know. When I partnered with Smiles Change Lives, however, everything changed.

News producers love stories about community service, access to care and especially children in need. When you focus on what you're doing for others, there's a much greater chance that local news stations take notice. In all honesty, news departments are hungry for feel-good stories that will resonate with the community. These stories are well-received and news stations enjoy producing them. When you leverage the power of publicity, you help make their job easier. Producers don't have to go out and look for a great story to share. Instead, you bring the story to them.

Many people don't realize that a lot of the news they see on television and in newspapers is generated through public relations efforts. I'm not referring to the type of "if it bleeds, it leads" stories. If someone has robbed a bank or committed a crime, that is going to get reported and it wasn't first generated by a public relations department. I'm referring to those stories that showcase someone in your community. They are stories that may include things like a doctor who is being interviewed about a new type of procedure, a cooking segment, or a business that bought the baseball team new dugouts.

Many of these stories are generated through publicity. How the process typically works is that a great press release is written and submitted to the appropriate person. They take it from there to either publish what you have given them, or they reach out to you for more information, to arrange a special segment, conduct interviews and more. That's how a lot of community news gets out there, and it's all quite effective at helping the business that is being highlighted.

Big Measures

I've used publicity as an important tool in helping to grow my practice. I'm not the only one who realizes how beneficial and necessary it is and why every practice should be taking advantage of it. Just about every kind of business on the planet can benefit from getting publicity, especially if it's something that helps to solidify your connection to the community and lets people know that you care and support them.

Bill Gates, one of the most successful business leaders and richest people to ever walk the planet, said "If I were down to my last dollar, I would spend it on public relations."

That's a significant statement. Of all the things he could spend that dollar on in order to help him get more money in return, he would spend it on public relations. That's because he has a thorough understanding of how important public relations is and what it can do to elevate a business and its position. Publicity can help give your practice the kind of reputation that makes people want to talk and refer others to you. I've gained countless new patients in this very way over the years.

In "The Seven Keys to Effective Marketing," a platform and system I've taught orthodontists for many years, I stress the importance of effective public relations. Unfortunately, most orthodontists are either too busy or simply unaware of the need for public relations in their practices. If that sounds like you, then know that you are not alone. But also know that you need to make a change. If you want to grow your business and establish an amazing reputation within your community, you need to grab onto public relations with both hands and let it lead you down the path toward success.

Richard Branson, charismatic billionaire and entrepreneur extraordinaire, nailed it when he said he'd much rather invest in a good PR story than he would in a front-page advertisement. He's right. Consider how much a front-page ad just about anywhere will cost you. They cost a lot, for starters, but I must go back to the fact that anything in that ad is something that you are saying. It's not something that is being said about you and your office.

Sure, you may get some referrals from it. That stands to reason. But you will never get the referrals and community connection from it that you can when you get publicity.

You've probably seen the ads on television for AT&T. In a series of clever spots, the company promotes the message that "Just OK is not OK." In one example, a tax specialist named Phil, who is undergoing his own IRS audit, promises a new client, "I'll get your taxes in an OK place." His desk has a photograph of his boat "Offshore Accounts" docked in the Cayman Islands and asks the client to call him by his new name, Dennis Celery, because Phil is "legally dead – fell off a boat." The customer wisely takes her business elsewhere.

In another example, a customer asks an auto mechanic if he is any good at repairing brakes.

The mechanic replies, "We're OK."

"Just, OK?" asks the customer.

The mechanic says, "We have a saying around here, if the brakes don't stop you, something else will."

These television ads are funny and examples range from carnival workers putting up new rides to a physician who has recently had his hospital privileges reinstated, about to take a patient to surgery. The message is clear. "Just OK is not OK," and your practice is no different. People expect you to be good at what you do. Otherwise, how in the world did you graduate from dental school and orthodontic residency?

But, to be really unique and to have people talk about your practice, you must be more than just "OK." You have to be more than plain old vanilla. You can achieve this by embracing SCL and having others talk about how great your practice is, how you are different and how you support the community.

What's In It For Me?

Except for your mother, your spouse and every other orthodontist on the planet, no one is really that interested in orthodontics. This might sting but it's true. Consumers are interested in what you can do for them, but only a small segment of any market is actively seeking an orthodontist at any given time. If you want to cast a broader net, you must make your story and what you do more appealing and you do that through effective public relations.

When you support your community or change the life of a child by giving them free orthodontic treatment, you are casting a wider net. There are many people who care about who does things in their community to help make it a better. People care about community support and who goes above and beyond. This is one of the reasons that working with Smiles Change Lives is so effective in providing a truly unique way to help grow your practice.

In working with Smiles Change Lives, you are truly changing the life of a child. Each time you do that, you are helping to make the world a better place. By providing one act of kindness at a time, we are strengthening our community. It's like the old saying goes that everyone thinks of changing the world but few people think of changing themselves. By being the change that we want in our community, we are playing an important role, setting the example, and strengthening the ties and reputation we have within our community.

You can't buy a great reputation, but it's certainly something you can earn. You earn a great reputation by showing you care and by supporting your community. You commit to changing the lives of children in need and in return, you'll receive a lot of publicity. But this publicity is not something you get for free. You earn it. You earn it by helping others. You earn it by supporting your community. You earn it by changing lives forever and in the world of marketing, advertising and growing referrals, it simply doesn't get any better than this.

Good Work Falls Short

Most people, including orthodontists, believe that if you do good work everything else will fall into place. They strive for more accolades, more experience, and try to prove to everyone that they do a good job. Well guess what, I'm here to tell you that being good at what you do is simply not enough. I know that comes as a shock to most people, but it's the truth. Being good is like being vanilla, and you already have an idea how I feel about practices that are simply vanilla. They won't ever become a huge success. Nothing vanilla ever does.

You need to go beyond just being good or being vanilla. So, why don't you become wildly successful by being good? Because that's the bare minimum of what you should be. Everyone already expects that as a professional you are good at what you do and that you are going to provide them with good service.

When did just meeting expectations ever help propel a business toward the top of their field? I'm going to go out on a limb here and say next to never. It doesn't happen. Those who are just meeting the expectations set forth by their patients will likely always remain stagnant in one place. Is that really where you want to be? I don't think so, or you wouldn't have picked up this book in the first place.

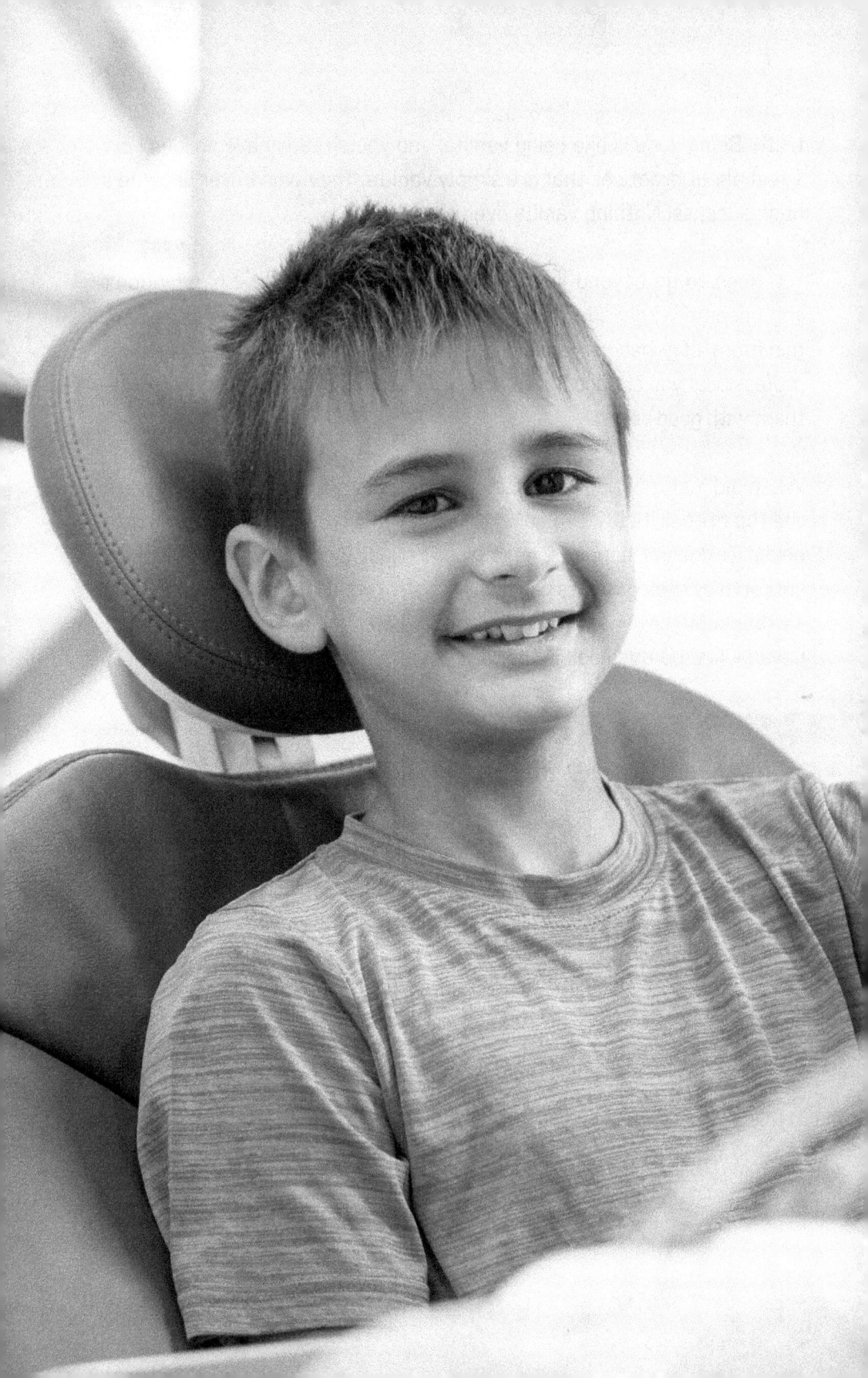

You must reach for more, be unique, and do something that people respect. Combine that with doing good work and you have a recipe for amazing success. Smiles Change Lives is a unique opportunity that people respect, so when it's combined with the great patient service that your team offers, you have a winning combination. It's worked for me, it's worked for other orthodontist offices around the country, and it will certainly work for you, too.

PR the Easy Way

Finding the time to dedicate yourself or someone on your team to public relations efforts can be time consuming. Anything in your office that is time consuming means that it is costly, too. Here's the real kicker: they may spend a lot of time trying to get you publicity and not get a single word in print, in television, or on radio. This can happen as a result of their efforts, what stories they are offering, or any number of other factors.

There are more people pushing publicity story ideas than there is news space to cover them all. Some are going to be chosen, others will sit on the back burner, and still others will never garner another look. You, of course, want your stories to be chosen. The chosen ones are those that will be highlighted, reach the people, and bring the benefits to your office.

So, what's the trick, how do you go about being the chosen one and also minimize your time spent on trying to obtain that PR? Well, in short, you do something unique. When you work with Smiles Change Lives, for example, you are doing something that is worthy of publicity. The media outlets in your area crave stories like that because the public loves them. They will typically jump at the chance to shed light on a story where an orthodontist has given free treatment to a child in need, because it's literally life changing.

Each time the media outlets grab hold of a story like that, they get to provide their audience with something enjoyable. For you, they show the people in your community how much you care about helping others, how you support them, how you change lives. You can't buy that kind of publicity. It has a profound impact on how your community sees your practice and relates to you. They see your office as a community partner, rather than someone who is just looking to get business. You have demonstrated that you have a vested interest in your community and in the people who are in it.

The SCL Publicity Approach

It's important that every orthodontist realize and appreciate the fact that they are not just providing treatment. They are providing an outcome. There's a big difference. People are not coming to your office because they want treatment. They are coming to you because they want an outcome. That outcome may be more confidence, to raise their self-esteem, or to love the smile they see when they look in the mirror.

Our job in the business is to deliver more service value than patients pay us in dollars and time and so that we can grow through referrals. In working with Smiles Change Lives, I always deliver more service value, and it has worked incredibly well to help grow my practice through referrals.

Smiles Change Lives realizes how valuable the publicity is that you can earn from providing treatment to children in need who pass their screening.

As such, they make it easier than you would imagine obtaining publicity. They handle it for you. This keeps your team from even having to get involved in reaching out to your local media. The Smiles Change Lives

OUR JOB IN THE BUSINESS IS TO DELIVER MORE SERVICE VALUE THAN PATIENTS PAY US IN DOLLARS SO THAT WE CAN GROW THROUGH REFERRALS.

team handles all aspects of reaching out to the media on your behalf. This is important, because once again I point to the fact that it's far more beneficial for someone else to say something about your office than for you to say it.

When SCL reaches out to the media on your behalf, they are letting them know that an orthodontist in the area is doing something amazing. They get them interested in learning more and sharing the information with their audience. You get the great publicity, but you didn't even have to be the one to do the work to contact the media. You just benefit from it. All you have to do is keep doing what you do, which is helping people obtain amazing smiles.

Every orthodontist that I've ever spoken with, and it's been a lot, wants to help those who are less fortunate. They want to use their skills to help change lives and provide treatment to those who may have difficulty paying to get their teeth fixed. They don't always know how to go about doing it, because it's difficult to screen people, decide who is worthy of the assistance, and then to try and let others know of the good deeds.

Smiles Change Lives has created a win-win-win program that benefits everyone it touches. The children in the program literally have their lives changed, because they get the treatment they need. They will go on to be more confident and reap the many rewards that come from having a great smile and high self-esteem. The parents win, because they were able to help their child get the treatment they need. The orthodontist who provided the treatment wins because they not only feel good about what they are doing by supporting that family, but they also get to help build a great reputation of having solid and caring ties with their community.

I like to refer to working with Smiles Change Lives as PR the smart way. That's because, going back to what I suggested earlier, it's working smarter, rather than harder. You don't have to increase your public relations efforts when you work with Smiles Change Lives. You simply provide the treatment to the selected patients and they handle the rest. You will gain all the benefits of having a great public relations team on your side who are armed with a sizzling hot story that the press will want to report on.

PR the smart way is all about taking advantage of the benefits that are there when you provide someone with free treatment. What you get in return is far more valuable than if you took out a front-page ad. It's more valuable than if you tried to get some free publicity on your own. I know, because my practice has greatly benefited from gaining publicity the smart way. I just keep doing what I do, treating the patients they send my way, and lo and behold - the media continues to put a spotlight on it.

Every spotlight that goes on the service work that we are doing in my practice is powerful. Yes, our team feels good about it, the practice grows immensely from it, and at the end of the day we have sent people out of our office who have a whole new feel for life. They love their teeth, they feel good about speaking with people, their confidence goes up, they are more willing to try out for clubs at school, and they no longer fear dating.

What we are doing when we work with the Smiles Change Lives program helps grow our business, but ultimately, we know that our efforts have quite literally changed the life of someone deserving. Everyone wants to do something meaningful for others, they just don't always know how to go about doing it. Now you do.

To download sample press releases and to see examples of stories that have been reported on my practices in the news, register your book for these free bonuses and more at:

www.SCLBookBonuses.com

"YOU WANT TO BE THE PEBBLE
IN THE POND THAT CREATES THE
RIPPLE FOR CHANGE." — TIM COOK, APPLE CEO

CHAPTER 3

WHY YOUR PATIENTS CARE ABOUT SMILES CHANGE LIVES

....

"The goal as a company is to have customer service that is not just the best but legendary." - Sam Walton

....

You probably enjoy donating to charities, helping those in need and supporting various causes in your community and beyond. Well, so do your patients and potential patients. It would be hard to find someone who didn't have a favorable opinion of people and businesses supporting their community. When you do it through your business, you are making a statement about your practice. That statement is that you care about the people in your community and you want to make it and the world a better place.

There is a good chance that you have a favorable opinion about some companies in part because of the charity work that they do as an extension to their main mission. Every successful company understands the benefits to philanthropy. They know that companies that are a huge success donate their time in big and meaningful ways. Whether through volunteer hours, donating money to support a cause, or by teaming up with a charity to help further their mission, by doing good there is a lot of good that comes back to them.

You've heard it said, "What goes around comes around." This holds true for companies that support their communities. When you do things to help others, you invest in people. You strengthen them and you help create a better society. Everyone wants to live in a better community, so instead of waiting around for someone else to make the positive change, do something big to make it happen.

There was research conducted not long ago that found that millennials – more so than other generations – have a favorable opinion of those businesses that support others.

Millennials tend to want to do business with those companies more than they would others, because of their charitable contributions to society. This is important to consider, because not only do they make up 25% of the population, but they will soon be making the decisions on where to take their own children for braces. If your practice is involved in helping others, that puts you in a higher category in their mind, and that alone could be the deciding factor on why they choose your office for treatment.

Making a Difference

I've long taught that people with money want to spend it with businesses that make a difference in their communities. You might not think of your patients and their parents as being "affluent," but let's face it – the people who utilize your services are largely spending elective dollars on a cosmetic procedure. I know you think you're saving lives one tooth at a time but outside the cleft palate patients, surgical (including canine impactions), TMD or complex restorative patients you treat, your patients aren't going to suffer harm if they forgo orthodontic treatment. None of your patients, even the complex cases, will ever have the word "malocclusion" written on their death certificate. Harsh and kind of dark, but true.

So, if patients are spending elective dollars on a healthcare procedure that is mostly cosmetic, all other factors being equal, why wouldn't they want to spend their hard-earned money on a provider who makes a big difference in the community? Hint: they do, and we have the data to support that.

In 2009, when I massively expanded my practice, we hired a brilliant third- party demographics and research firm to interview over 10,000 families in the Kansas City area and asked them what was most important when choosing an orthodontist. Trust was first, convenience was second and price was third. Inside the category of trust, way ahead of board certifications or graduating from a specific institution (all the things we, as orthodontists, think are important), consumers said the following three factors would elevate the level of trust in their eyes when deciding on an orthodontist for their family: doctors who run on time, have excellent reviews, and stand behind their work with a satisfaction guarantee led the list.

In addition, parents also placed higher trust in doctors who supported philanthropic organizations in their community and donated their time to help underserved children.

This phenomenon is not limited to orthodontics. Companies across all industries and niches are viewed as more trustworthy when they fulfill the promises they make to customers and are actively seen doing good in their communities. The NFL and NBA have latched onto this concept with active PR initiatives and millions of dollars of charity work and donations poured into communities that often support the teams with tax dollars, bond initiatives, and new stadiums. These large, successful organizations are pleased to help others, but they're also monitoring the effectiveness of these efforts. Trust me. They would drop these initiatives in a heartbeat if they had data that suggested it decreased trust in the community and in their fan base.

Later in chapter seven, we'll talk about the transformation this can make in the new patient room and in your employees' ability to see a more abundant world and a higher sense of purpose. For now, let's look at some great examples of how other smart companies leverage philanthropy to enhance their image in the public eye.

Companies that Stand Out

Successful companies know that it pays to team up with a charitable cause. Whether they are donating money, giving their time through volunteer hours, providing free services, or doing something else to make the connection, they know it's good business. Anytime a business has strong bonds with philanthropy, they will elevate their reputation in the community which will give them more business in the long run.

Bill Gates is not only one of the wealthiest people in the world, but also known as one of the most charitable. He has donated tens of billions of dollars through The Bill and Melinda Gates Foundation to various causes all over the world, with the goal of improving healthcare and relieving poverty. The company that he founded, Microsoft, also embodies this spirit of giving and often makes the list of the most charitable companies in the United States. According to company records, they donate over $2 million dollars a day in cash and equipment all over the world to help people become self-sufficient. Through the company's philanthropy division, their mission is to empower others by providing them with educational opportunities, especially in rural areas where people often get left behind due to lack of resources. This valuable education teaches in-demand skills and strengthens the labor market, which continues to reward more lucrative jobs to those with backgrounds in computer science.

Since the inception of this branch of the company in 2016, Microsoft Philanthropies has provided over $1.2 billion dollars in cash grants and technology and supported over 200,000 non-profit organizations all over the planet. One of their largest endeavors has been to bring high-speed Internet to rural communities including many remote parts of the United States. It is estimated that over 2 million Americans have benefited from this access thus far, and it has provided new opportunities which will continue to bring benefits well after the project is complete.

Without the charitable contributions that Microsoft makes, people would see them as just another technology company. However, their track record of over 30 years of generosity has not only earned them an excellent reputation as a "great company" but it has brought them tremendous success.

Cisco, the technology company, is another one that is known for their charity work. They support the community and they do so in a huge way. In fact, their contributions have come to over $286 million thus far. They believe in supporting local charities so much so that they give each of their employees five paid days off per year to use for volunteering services. Keep in mind that they have over 73,000 employees throughout the world. That quickly adds up to a lot of money paid to employees who are out volunteering for charity, and it adds up to a lot of help that charities are receiving from Cisco employees.

Add to those volunteer hours the fact that Cisco will also match any funds that their employees donate to nonprofit organizations. This encourages their many employees to also take a personal interest in their community. The employees can feel good knowing that they are not only donating some of their time to make a difference but they are also helping the cause financially. They also get to choose the charity that they volunteer for and support. This is huge, because it gives every employee the power to help their community where they see fit.

At the end of the day, Cisco is making a huge impact when it comes to charitable services. They have 73,000 people on the streets who, in the name of Cisco, are donating hours of their time, as well as donating financially. Collectively, they are working together to help make the world a better place, strengthen their bond with their communities, and they are elevating their company image across the board. It's hard to not love that they are doing so much for charities. We can all agree that what they are doing is meaningful, impactful, and overall a good thing.

Another company that has done a great job of digging in and connecting with their community is Target. The big box store has made local ties in all the communities they are in through some of the programs they have put in place for that very reason. All total, the company to date has given over $217 million in cash and products. While they are giving some larger donations, it's often the smaller ones that are going to have a big impact on their local community.

Big box retailer Target reaches people locally by giving grants for school field trips and sports. Many schools are financially at a disadvantage when it comes to taking kids on field trips, so they can apply for a $700 grant from Target that can be used for this purpose. They have also paid for many kids to take those field trips. Not only is this is greatly appreciated by the children, but also by the teachers, parents and field trip destinations. Thus, growing Target's impact beyond just the classroom and giving more and more people the opportunity to say nice things about them. Additionally, they offer grants for children who want to play soccer, in which Target pays 100% for registration fees, player equipment, field equipment, and any professional development training that recipients may need to play for a season.

Imagine in your community you know that Target is paying for kids to go on school field trips and is picking up the tab for some kids to play soccer. These are positive attributes that are going to help create happier kids who will most likely go on to do better in life. That's a win-win for the business image as well as for the community. Anytime a business takes measures to improve the life of a child or someone in the community, they are helping to make it a better place. Even touching the life of one person in a meaningful way can go on to have a huge impact on the community. There's a ripple effect where you touch one life and they go on to touch one and it continues from there.

Whenever there is a disaster, there are always big-name companies that reach out and make large donations. Their efforts may be financial contributions, they may donate truckloads of products, or even offer up employees for volunteer efforts. Consider Hurricane Michael, which hit the Florida panhandle hard and caused widespread destruction. When that happened, there were large companies that quickly offered aid.

The Walt Disney Company, Google, and Apple each donated $1 million. JC Penney and the Yankees both donated $100,000 each. The list goes on and on of businesses that made donations to help the community. Companies were quick to provide cash donations, send truckloads of products, and to send people who could lend a helping hand. Why did they do all of this? For starters, because they care about people, as we all do, and they want to help those in need, especially if they have the means. Whether you are providing someone with the diapers their child needs or you are giving someone a hand up by helping them to get the orthodontic care they need, you are connecting with the community.

When you connect with your community, there are wonderful things that come back to you and your team.

A great local story of how a company has reached success by having strong ties to the community is Gallery Furniture in Houston, Texas. The company has been in business for over 37 years and has always had a strong commitment to supporting their community. They have sponsored events, given furniture to families in need, and helped in a multitude of ways. Their most heartfelt contribution came when Houston was hit by Hurricane Harvey, leaving many people homeless. The furniture store opened several locations, turning them into shelters for those who needed a place to stay. The people were invited to stay there and sleep on the furniture in the store. Thousands of people took them up on the offer.

The owner of Gallery Furniture, Jim McIngvale, made such a big impact on the community with his generosity that a petition was started to proclaim a day in his honor and give him the key to the city. When the petition closed it had well over 200,000 signatures. That's a community that loves Gallery Furniture for its strong commitment to helping others.

Where do you think the people of Houston will go when they need new furniture? The company's image is so strong and positive that the first place they look will be Gallery Furniture. And the outpouring of positive media he and the company received following his contribution to helping those in his city reached around the globe.

Some orthodontists reading this may think: "These stories are great, but our practice is not Microsoft or Target sized. Even if I treated a couple of Smiles Change Lives kids every month, I wouldn't make much of a difference."

That is simply not true.

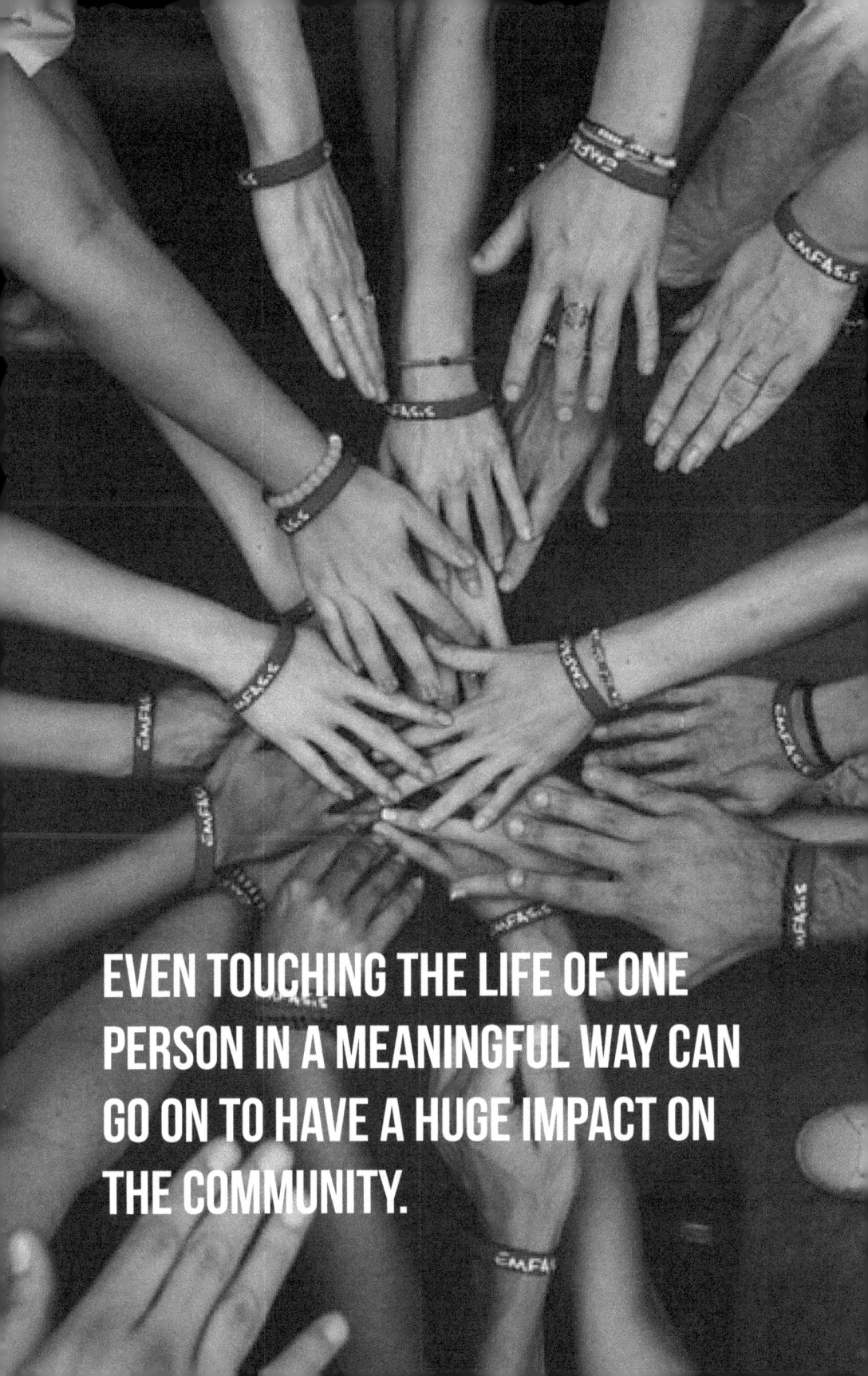

EVEN TOUCHING THE LIFE OF ONE PERSON IN A MEANINGFUL WAY CAN GO ON TO HAVE A HUGE IMPACT ON THE COMMUNITY.

Every child that receives treatment through Smiles Change Lives receives an enormous benefit, and if you have the ability to change the life of just one person...why wouldn't you want to embrace that opportunity? Each orthodontist that participates in the program is a key part of a huge result, and working together, you are treating children who would otherwise not get this type of help. Therefore anyone that participates IS in fact, making a huge difference.

Helping Many or Focusing on One

I've often shared my thoughts about whether you should try to help many charities or focus on giving one contribution to a single charity or cause. I'm a fan of focusing your efforts on one cause and for good reason. When you try to give to numerous charities, your efforts will have to be split, so you will be giving less to each. This means that your impact will not be as great, nor as noticed by those in the community. The smaller contributions you make to numerous causes may not even register on the radar because they are small and so spread out. Yet when you focus on one cause or charity you can make a significant difference.

By working with Smiles Change Lives, you and your team become a part of something much bigger than the few kids you might treat each year. Our impact when we go it alone is small, but when we join together and work with Smiles Change Lives, the whole is greater than the sum of our parts. Let's say you work with four kids per year in the program. Yes, you do change the lives of these kids forever. However, at the same time you and your employees can contribute to something across your city, state and entire nation, which adds up to millions in donated care and thousands of lives changed. The ripple effect you help put into motion will keep going and expanding and this is an extremely exciting and motivating truth about working with SCL. Remind your team and your community leaders of this and don't be shy about promoting the good you're doing in your city and through your affiliation with the entire organization, the change you're helping to create across the nation too. Let's say that in one year you have $10,000 that you can donate in cash or services. If you split that up among numerous causes or charities, each will get maybe $2,000 each. There's not a whole lot they can do with that amount. They need a lot of other people to make similar contributions, so that they can have enough to make some sort of impact. On the other side, what kind of impact could you have if you gave all that cash or services contribution to one single charity or cause? You would make a meaningful impact. Not only that, but your office would become known for aligning with that charity and making a difference.

When you choose one cause or charity to team up with, your efforts won't go unnoticed. In fact, quite the opposite will happen. Your efforts will be spotlighted, noticed more, and you will become known as the orthodontist who supports families that need a hand up. Your office is the one that helps your community by changing lives, one smile at a time. That's a contribution that your office will benefit from, your staff will feel good about, the families will be grateful for, and the community will reward you for.

You probably have that little voice in your head that is saying you are not supposed to be rewarded for helping others, right? Forget that little voice. Are you eager to be rich? Do you want your business to be wildly successful? Then you must be willing to come to terms with the fact that it's not only perfectly fine for you to reap the rewards for helping others in your community, but that it's a good thing. As I've pointed out already, it's a win-win situation for everyone. If you want your business to be a huge success, you must consider unique ways to get there. Let your competitor turn away from leveraging the power of charity work.

In my practice, I've always been eager to be rich, and I'm not afraid to say it. I don't think being rich or making a lot of money for what I do is an evil or bad thing. I wouldn't have made it to the top, becoming the highest paid orthodontic consultant on the planet, if I worried about what my peers thought of my tactics. I want my practice to be wildly successful and I want my patients to be supremely happy. I've worked hard to achieve both things and I have no guilt about reaping the rewards.

Seeking Stability

There are a lot of important lessons I've learned about money over the years in my quest to obtain it and become as successful as I can. One of the things I've learned is that money is attracted to complexity in business stability.

What that means is that in your practice, you must have many types of revenue streams and lots of sources for new patients. In other words, you can't have all your eggs in one basket, as the saying goes.

If you focus on one thing in your practice, you become vulnerable, because conditions change. Nothing stays the same and as things change and evolve, your business model can be left behind if you don't have a diverse way to reach your target market and you don't have diversity in what you offer. By having more complexity in your practice, you are helping to ensure that if one string is tugged on, the whole ball of yarn doesn't come unraveled.

I'm not shy about letting people know that one of the beautiful aspects of working with Smiles Change Lives is that it brings me new patients. And I'm not referring to the patients I provide pro-bono treatment to. I'm referring to the stream of referrals I get as a result of donating time to help the patients they send my way. It has helped to provide my practice with a layer of complexity in how I obtain new referrals that would otherwise be difficult to achieve.

Spreading Good

As an orthodontist, you know how important straight teeth are. They can make a world of difference in someone's life. When people have finished treatment, they feel better about themselves, they are not afraid to go after the things they want, and they are more likely to be hired for jobs. It's an important responsibility, especially when you do it for someone who needs a hand up and may not otherwise be able to obtain treatment. As orthodontists, we are in a unique position, because we really can take action that will help make the world a better place, one smile at a time.

Like many other orthodontists, you likely have a passion for straightening teeth. Richard Branson, the founder of Virgin Group, multi-billionaire, and wildly successful businessman, once said "There is no greater thing you can do with your life and your work than to follow your passion – in a way that serves the world and you." When you work with a group like Smiles Change Lives, that's exactly what you are doing. You are using your life and your work to follow your passion in a way that is serving both you and the world. It doesn't get much better than that.

CHAPTER 4

HOW SMILES CHANGE LIVES CAN HELP YOUR REFERRING DOCTORS

"You can make more friends in two months by becoming interested in other people than you can in two years by trying to get other people interested in you."
- Dale Carnegie

As an orthodontist, you know how important referring doctors are to the success of your practice. If you don't know this already, then you will by the time you finish this chapter. And, hopefully you will never look at referring doctors in quite the same way once you have read this chapter. They have the power to play an important role in your practice's success. But it is also a two-way street in which you can play a role in their success. Many people don't realize this, but when you work with the Smiles Change Lives program, you can make an impact with referring dentists, too.

You might be surprised to hear that Smiles Change Lives can help your referring doctors. When you leverage the power of Smiles Change Lives and your referring dentists, you'll make a bigger impact, serve more patients in need and find even more good ripples come back your way.

Beyond Your Office

The benefits of Smiles Change Lives extend far beyond the patients and your practice. Far beyond your employees and your public relations. Smiles Change Lives can even help your referring doctors. Dentists, oral surgeons, and physicians can all benefit when they refer potential patients to your office or directly to Smiles Change Lives, as many of these families become cash-paying patients in these practices. Some of your referral network will opt to treat these patients for free, deriving all the same benefits you and I derive when we treat orthodontic cases for free. But, even if your referral network doesn't want to treat any pro-bono cases, the amount of attention they will receive for being affiliated with Smiles Change Lives is tremendous.

For many years, I've shipped a small gift to any doctor who starts treating patients in the Smiles Change Lives program. The gift includes a little welcome note from me, and a USB thumb drive pre-loaded with all the resources I've used to host events, get on the news, send press releases and enhance my public image, all through my affiliation with Smiles Change Lives.

If you would like to request this gift for your own office and for those doctors in your referral network, simply send a note to my office via support@burlesonseminars.com or call us at 800-891-7520 and be sure to ask for the Smiles Change Lives Provider Welcome Kit. It's my pleasure to pay it forward and send this gift to you, absolutely free.

I'll never forget when I asked my friend, an oral surgeon, if he would be willing to take a few cases in the Smiles program and do their extractions for free. Many of our Smiles kids have severe malocclusion and severe crowding. Although I extract teeth in fewer than 10% of my fee-for-service patients, nearly 50% of my Smiles kids need extractions.

This surgeon was nice enough to take on a few cases each year, but he noticed the more he took, the more his staff proudly promoted his charity work, and before we knew it, he was featured in a news report with the local dental society. Today his office is the go-to office where not only patients want to be treated but also surgical assistants want to work. He sees a bigger vision for his life and his practice. He has attached his team to a higher sense of purpose, and he sees the world with abundance, not scarcity.

What if you could find one or two referring colleagues who changed their lives and their practice forever simply through their association with you and your dedication to Smiles Change Lives? Do you think that doctor might refer to you for life? I think so.

When you refer someone to have extractions and they get the love and respect from people in their community for doing the work, you will have helped them in a huge way. They are going to find that they get the media attention, the parents will respect and refer them, and the word will get around that they are doing pro-bono work. While the dentist thought their office was merely doing a necessary extraction in working with you, what they will get out of the relationship is far more than that. When they see what they get out of it, they will be more likely to think favorably of your office and want to send more referrals your way as a result.

Doctor Referrals Rock

In our line of work, it is crucial that we make solid connections with the dentists who work in our community. What is also important to realize is that this is a relationship that can and should work both ways. Your mission is to cultivate good, strong relationships with the dentists in your area so that you both mutually benefit from working together. As I've mentioned before, it is crucial that your referral sources be diversified. You don't want all your referrals coming from one place. Having multiple sources of referrals will ensure your success.

If you haven't reached out to dentists in your community to create a strong relationship, there's a good chance you're missing an excellent opportunity. See each dentist in your community as an asset and valuable resource that can help your practice grow. Be a valuable resource and asset to their practice as well. When you give first and show interest in their success, you'll draw amazing people to you like a magnet and help everyone around you thrive.

Higher Sense of Purpose

If you want a great way to engage your team to provide the best service around, you want to appeal to their desire to contribute to a higher sense of purpose. Most employees enjoy their job, but they crave being connected to something bigger and more meaningful. They want what they do to make a significant difference in people's lives. Sure, they are doing that with every patient they take care of, but there's something special and profoundly impactful about providing care to someone who wouldn't have otherwise been able to afford it.

When you refer your Smiles Change Lives patients to select dentist offices, you are doing their practice a tremendous favor. They may not see it right away and possibly even wonder why they should get involved. But once they take on the challenge and become immersed in being a part of the program by providing treatment to your Smiles Change Lives patients, they will see and feel the major difference your connection with them has made.

Remember all the love and support that was mentioned that you get as a provider for Smiles Change Lives patients? Well, they will feel that same love from the community. And they will feel it because you brought it to them. Your office will have personally hand-selected which dentist office is going to be the fortunate one to get showered with all the publicity and community attention for taking part in supporting others. This is something that the dentist is going to fully appreciate, and once their office has done it, they will want to do even more of it, but it's also going to touch their employees in a big way.

All employees want to contribute to the greater good. Yours, mine, and the dentist office down the block. People feel good about helping others. They want to feel their work and contribution is important in helping to make a difference. When you send a Smiles Change Lives patient their way, you will be helping their entire team feel good. They will know they are contributing to something significant, important, and life changing. That's a feeling that is going to transcend into every area of their work.

Employees who feel they are contributing to the greater good or helping with a higher sense of purpose are more likely to be engaged. They will want to go the extra mile for all your patients, provide the best service around, and will feel that they are working for the best dentist office on the planet. That's because they are not just there to perform dental work on people who have the money or insurance to get the work done. They are there to help those who need a hand up. They are there to help change lives, one smile at a time. That's a feeling that is hard to beat and one that they will want to keep.

When someone feels good about what they are doing, they will want to keep doing it. In order to make that happen, they will look to your office to keep being the office that helps with those Smiles Change Lives patients who need extractions. They will actively strengthen the bond that they have with your office. How will they do that? There is no better way they can do that than to send referrals your way. The greatest possible way for a dentist to show you appreciation and to solidify your relationship with their office is to keep the referrals going.

Dentists who work with you on Smiles Change Lives patients will want to continue doing so. They will love what they get in return from working with those patients, which is more business and love from the

community, and they will keep the circle of positivity going by passing that on to your office. Your efforts of working with these select patients will be helping far more people than just the patient who sits down in your chair. Your efforts have a ripple effect that will go out and help many others by touching so many people's lives.

Gallup conducted a survey regarding employee engagement and shared their results. They reported that, "A highly engaged workforce means the difference between a company that outperforms its competitors and one that fails to grow." Read that statement again, and let it sink in. It's imperative for the growth of your practice that you have highly engaged employees. Your practice's success is dependent upon it. That's how important employee engagement is.

In Gallup's report, they shed light on the employee engagement issue. They found that 87% of workers are not engaged, yet most employers are not even aware of it. This means your practice may not be as successful as you'd like it to be, simply because your team is not engaged, and you haven't even noticed it. The same can be said for the referring dentists you work with. Here's another statistic they gave from their report that needs to sink in. They state that companies who have highly engaged workforces outperform their peers by 147% in earnings per share. That's huge, and it makes a significant financial difference in your office, as well as the referring dentist offices you work with.

One major way to engage your team and a way that your referring doctors can engage their team is for them to feel they are contributing to a higher sense of purpose. They want to feel as though they are doing something huge, making a difference in the world, and helping people beyond the basics that they are supposed to be doing in that role. When they get a chance to do more, team up to give a hand up, then the engagement is going to go up. That leads to better service, a better practice, and significant growth.

Growing Your Referral Base

Your referral base is akin to oxygen when it comes to your practice. It's one of the most important tools you can have and, if done correctly. it will help to ensure your company's success. It's such an important topic that I wrote a whole book on it, I've written about it in my newsletters, and I have spoken about it in my seminars. It's that important and something that cannot be overlooked or undervalued if you want to be a huge success.

When you diversify where you get your referrals from, you will be doing a great thing for your practice. You need your referrals to come to you from a variety of ways and directions. The more ways you have them coming to you, the better. This is one of the beautiful aspects of working with Smiles Change Lives. When you work with their patients, you will get many referrals from the work that you have done. But you will also be helping your referring doctors as well.

Many doctors you work with to whom you send Smiles Change Lives patients will gain the same type of community publicity that you receive. They will be a part of a special network of professionals who are working together for the good of people in the community. Their image and reputation will be elevated, the people they work with will want to go back to their office and refer others to them, and more people will choose to make appointments with that office over their competitor. Plus, just as your office will, they will reap the rewards of having a team that is more engaged and feels good about being a part of something bigger and more important.

When your efforts have brought so much to your referring doctors, it will not go unnoticed. Guess who they will be referring their patients to who need braces? You guessed it: Those patients will be sent your way. Thus, you will be increasing your referrals, too.

The Smiles Change Lives program is one that will help everyone involved. Good things come to all those who are involved and touched by it. I don't say that simply to promote the organization. I say this and all the other great things I say about it because I truly believe in it. I know what working with this program can do for your practice and that of your referring doctors, because I've seen it in action. I have seen how powerful the aura is for those who are involved in helping these children out.

Sharing Success Secrets

Many orthodontists or professionals who are at the top of their field would prefer to keep their secrets to themselves. They don't want to share with their peers how they got to the top. They fear that in doing so they may lose a little bit themselves. Once they have found something special that works, they want to hold on tight, tap it for all it's worth,

IF YOU WANT A GREAT WAY TO
ENGAGE YOUR TEAM AND GET THEM
PROVIDING THE BEST SERVICE
AROUND, YOU WILL WANT TO APPEAL
TO THEIR DESIRE TO CONTRIBUTE TO
A HIGHER SENSE OF PURPOSE.

and keep it under lock and key. I'm not like that. I have never been like that and never will.

I personally would love to see every orthodontist and every dentist rise to the top. As a field, I want us all to succeed. There is room at the top for everyone to do well, and I want us to all do well. I want to be rich for sharing my passion helping to straighten teeth, and I want you all to experience the same. Therefore, I share my secrets to success.
Not only do I share my secrets to success, but I've done it countless times and in numerous ways. I've essentially given every orthodontist on the planet the blueprints to how to have an incredibly successful practice. I hold nothing back, because I want us all to succeed. I share what has worked for me, what has fallen flat on its face, my ups and downs, my successes and failures, all in the hopes that it will help someone else to rise to the top. I hope that everyone who reads my books, newsletters, or listens to my seminars takes everything to heart and learns from my experiences.

I speak so highly of the Smiles Change Lives program because I can say unequivocally that it has been a wonderful thing for my practice. It has helped my team feel great about what they do, it has brought my office a lot of free publicity, and it has helped demonstrate how much I care about my community. It has also helped to grow my referral network, as well as helped me to strengthen relationships with referring doctors. It has also helped those referring doctors build their own referrals, and build a team who feels good about what they are doing.

There are so many great things that can be said about the Smiles Change Lives program. Yet people would be hard pressed to come up with some cons to working with the program and in helping these young people out so they can go on to have straight teeth and more confidence in their life. Perhaps you feel that you may upset other orthodontists in your area because you will be in the limelight for doing something so good.

They may grow to be jealous of you because your office will grow and your level of success will climb. So what?

Let me be the first to tell you that I've had my share of setbacks, failures, and challenges. Through it all, I have emerged successful, although I guarantee you it was not without lots of scrapes and bruises. I've had my entire staff walk out on me on a cold February day in 2009. The moral of the story was that I deserved it. I had spent my time building a business where I was hell-bent on making everything perfect for the patient, but I forgot about the employees. They were still handling all our systems manually, as I hadn't taken the time or interest in automating anything yet. I'll be honest in saying that I didn't even know what InfusionSoft (a CRM system, now known as Keap) was at the time. I went from that to now being one of the world's highest paid InfusionSoft and marketing automation experts for healthcare practices.

I've spent years learning what works and what doesn't. I've made mistakes and I've learned from every one of them. I have used everything I have learned along the way to continue to grow my practice. But I didn't stop there, I have also used that information and my experiences to help countless other orthodontists around the country to grow their practice too. I didn't want to just stop with helping myself; I want and have a burning desire to help others in the field as well. I want myself to succeed, and I want you to do the same.

Smiles Change Lives isn't the only key to achieving practice success, but it's a critical tool that can help you and your referring dentists stand out from the competition. I've consistently seen these relationships result in stronger referral patterns and better care for our patients in the program. When it comes to success and the amazing benefits of Smiles Change Lives, don't be afraid to share the good news with your referring doctors and help everyone around you thrive.

CHAPTER 5:

THE CAPACITY MYTH

. . . .

"Take an old concept...and just put a new spin on
it, success will follow you like a shadow."
– Sheldon Adelson

. . . .

If you are like the rest of us, you have a number in mind regarding how many patients your office can manage treating. We all do. The problem is that over the years, I have learned that perceived number is dead wrong. What your true capacity is, or the number of people your office can treat and what you happen to think it may be are two totally different numbers.

You probably wonder how I can even say that. After all, I've never stepped foot in your office, and I don't know what's going on there, right? Wrong.

The truth is that I probably know more about how your office is, or should be, running than you do. I know this through my own years of experience, and also from my time spent working in the trenches, consulting other orthodontists around the country.

I've spent countless hours working with doctors who fly from around the world to my offices in Kansas City, helping them identify where they need to change. By doing this, I've helped them quickly double or triple the business and become more successful than they dreamed possible.

But I've also picked up a lot of information along the way when it comes to how people are running their practices and what can be done to change it. I know most practices are not at capacity, because I've seen it firsthand. It's all a myth.

Not only is it what I refer to as the capacity myth, but if you believe it and are running your practice according to it, then it's holding you back.
Self Limitation

One of the most common excuses I hear from orthodontists who only take one child per year (or no children) in the Smiles Change Lives program is that they simply don't have the capacity.

This is a limited mindset.

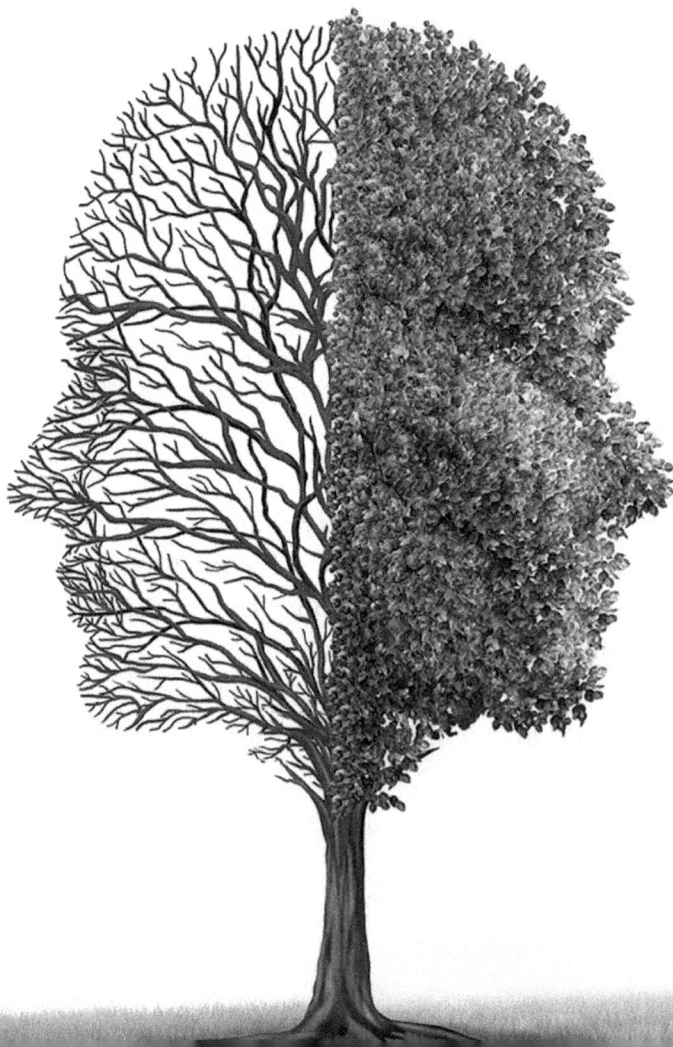

SMILES CHANGE LIVES : THE SMART ORTHODONTIST'S GUIDE TO GROWING A PURPOSE-DRIVEN PRACTICE

Based on our data from over 60,000 phone calls per month for our clients and privately held practices, listening and ranking all of these calls and observing the clinical statistics for our clients, I've only met one orthodontist who was running at true capacity, and we quickly recommended he get a bigger facility so that he and his team could continue to delight more patients.

Almost everyone has room in their schedule and if they don't, I quickly open more hours in the evening, early morning and weekends and/or raise their prices in order to solve true capacity problems.

In a study done in 2017 by the Journal of Clinical Orthodontics, it was determined that a full time (40 hours) solo orthodontic practice with 7 employees sees an average of 43 patients a day, It was also determined that the average patient appointment time is about 45 minutes per patient.

Using these data:

8 hours per day times 7 employees equals 56 hours per day. When you take 43 patients per day and multiply that by 45 minutes, you get 1935 minutes, or 32.25 hours.

Some assumptions should be made that one of those 7 employees is purely administrative, and that each employee gets one hour for lunch each day. You also need to consider one hour per day which is used for office setup and putting away tasks at the end of the day.

This adjusts your figures as follows: Administrative employee - 8 hours, lunch for remaining employees - 6 hours, and one additional 1 hour per day for setup and put away. **This leaves you a total of 20 hours.**

56 hours - 20 hours = 36 clinical hours per day. When you subtract 32.25 hours of treatment time, that leaves you with 3.75 hours each day of unproductive time.

This may seem like a lot when looking at figures, but in this same study it was determined that over 75% of the participants in the study stated that they felt they were "...not busy enough" and did not feel overworked.

From a numbers standpoint, 3.75 hours a day of unproductive time, times five times a week, times 50 weeks per year gives you 937.5 hours per year.

Here's how all of this fits in with treating Smiles Change Lives patients: Assuming you see one SCL patient at the previously determined average of 45 minutes, that's 540 minutes when multiplied by 12 months, or 8 hours.

Using this calculation for six SCL patients in this same equation, you get 3,240 minutes, or 54 hours.

Using this information, you can see why capacity is in fact a myth we've put in our heads because we think it's "too expensive" to treat Smiles Change Lives patients for free. Hogwash.

When looking at real data based on extensive study of how orthodontic practices are using their income and time, the most logical conclusion that one can come to is that SCL providers are not taking more of these patients because they either do not clearly understand the benefits and opportunity associated with participating, or because they don't want to participate.

One simply cannot accurately stand by the argument that insufficient time exists to treat SCL patients.

Another point that should be noted is that SCL patient hardware is provided at no out-of-pocket cost to the orthodontic practice. Also - these patients agree to come during your non-peak hours when accepted into the SCL program. Ask me how I know. I treat hundreds of Smiles Change Lives patients each year, and I also see more new patients in a single day than most orthodontists see in a month. I think the two are correlated.

The more generous I am with my time, energy, human capital and skills, the more the universe seems to reward me with patients (both cash paying and Smiles Change Lives) who appreciate what I do and want to tell their friends and family about me.

I'm a firm believer that my support of the community is absolutely related to the level of success that I have achieved. When you support others in your community, your community can't help but to come back and support you as well. Without even focusing on that aspect of it, that's exactly what happens. We focus on giving and in return we end up receiving.

It's a wonderful concept that changes the world for the better, one smile at a time.

Giving Back, Getting More

Entrepreneurs don't support those in their community or around the nation simply hoping to get something in return. They do it for several reasons. They know that it's good for morale within their office, they know their customers and patients appreciate it, and they know that it helps to strengthen their relationships. It shows people that they are a company that cares, it's not just all about them and what they want. They reach out to others and try to make the community a better place.

While you don't support others in hopes of getting something in return, that is typically what happens. It's how the universe works. What you give, you get back. What goes around comes around. That type of thing. What you send out to the world is what comes back to you. So, when you send out generosity, caring, and being helpful, the people in your community end up giving you back the same thing. They end up caring about your office. They want to be generous and send people your way, and they want to be helpful.

The bottom line is that helping others is almost always a win-win for everyone involved.
Take, for example, the free haircuts that some popular salons give out each year. They are busy, too. Anytime you go by a place like Great Clips, you are bound to see they are busy, with people waiting in the chairs for the haircuts. Yet they still find the time every year to help, and they do so in a big way. Every year, for Veteran's Day, they offer all veterans a free haircut.
They do this to thank them for their service.

Great Clips started the program in 2013 with a mission of wanting to support their community. Each year, they have offered up the free haircuts to all veterans and active duty service members on Veteran's Day. To date, they have given away over a million haircuts. Talk about being busy. It takes a lot of time to do a million haircuts. Yet the program continues to go on and is stronger than ever. They have even taken it a step further, giving all their non-veteran customers who get a haircut on that day a "pay it forward" card that they can give to a veteran. The veteran who receives the card can get a free haircut anytime from Veteran's Day through the end of the calendar year.

Why would this company give away over a million haircuts? They are busy, there's no doubt about it. Yet they still find the time to do it. Well, in giving the free haircuts, they immediately make a statement that they

support our veterans. Who doesn't love that? You immediately respect the fact that they are doing something for our veterans and active duty military members. By supporting our military, they help to elevate their public image and garner more respect.

In doing so, they also get back in a big way, whether it was their intention or not. In 2017, the company saw a 2.8 percent growth and expected a 7 percent growth the following year. During that one year alone, they did 106 million haircuts. Their company-wide revenue is now topping $1.5 billion per year. Clearly, they are also being rewarded. The veterans and active military members who receive haircuts for free are more likely to go back and pay for their next one. Those who go there and those who don't will have a favorable opinion about Great Clips, which makes them more likely to go there for haircuts and to recommend the place to others.

It's a win-win situation no matter how you look at it. When we give, we all end up winning.

That's just one example of a company supporting their community and how it has helped them to grow as a business. There are many more. Each year, there are companies around the nation that help others in one way or another. They are all busy and could easily brush the idea off, saying they don't have the time or inclination to engage in something like that. Rather than give excuses, however, they embrace the idea and become fully engaged.

There's an important reason why millions of companies around the country support their community or a cause. Sure, it makes them feel good, but as I've pointed out and experienced in my own practice, it does far more than that. It will help give your business an amazing reputation and you will get referrals coming your way with ease. People will want to refer your office, because they believe in what you are doing and what you stand for, and they will want to support you back.

There are some companies that engage in philanthropy work merely to help their corporate image. And again, this is a win-win for everyone involved, so there's nothing wrong with that approach.

Exxon Mobil, for example, takes a lot of heat when it comes to the environment, but in return they have given millions of dollars to fight malaria and help women in third world countries. Many people give Walmart a hard time for their cost-cutting ways, but they are also big contributors in trying to protect wilderness areas around the country.

There are doctors that donate their time and services, restaurants that give away free meals, and lawyers that represent people pro bono. Every one of these people and their offices is busy or could be busy doing something else. They could refuse the idea of philanthropy and say that they don't have the time or could do something more productive or lucrative. But when it comes down to it, those excuses are all just that, excuses, which contribute to the capacity myth.

One of the best things you can do for your practice is to support your community and let them see you doing it. As a big fan of the Smiles

Change Lives program and as someone whose office has greatly benefited from participating in it, I can say definitively that the Smiles Change Lives program is a solid choice when it comes to deciding where and how to give back.

Motivating Your Team Regarding Capacity

Right about now, you may be thinking that there is no way your team is going to go for this. They won't see how they can fit in Smiles Change Lives patients into what they feel is an already busy day. It's your job to help motivate them and give them a different vision. As the leader of your team, you are akin to the coach on the soccer field, or whatever your sport of choice is. Perhaps your team is out there busting their hump, working hard, and thinking they are doing all they can do. What's a coach to do?

A great coach calls them aside and points out that although they are working hard, they haven't won the game. Until the time comes that they do, they need to dig deep. They need to find it within themselves to step up, contribute more, and pull together to make things happen. It's your job being in the lead to help them see the rewards that will be there when they do step it up. A great leader brings out the best qualities in every one of their team members. They can identify where each of their strengths and weaknesses are and help them capitalize on their stronger assets in order to become a more valuable team player. And great coaches can do all of this in a way that is not condescending or makes the team members feel they are receiving criticism.

Employees may feel their day is busy already, but once you point out that there is always time to help, they will begin finding ways to make it happen. Plus, they will personally gain from the experience. A report in an issue of Harvard Business Review explained how altruism, or selflessness, helps boost employee performance. They explain that employees are highly motivated by a desire to provide something good to the world. Not just that, but employees are routinely seeking out employers who will let them do this while on company time.

People want to help and make the world a better place. But trust me when I say, many of them are busier outside work than when they are putting their time in at the office. Once they clock out, their evening is on full force and filled with one task after another. They must commute, pick up the kids, prepare meals, do laundry, get the kids to sports practice, and a host of other everyday type duties that we call life. Where exactly do they have the time to volunteer? Most of them don't have the time, despite having the desire.

When you have a program in-house that allows your employees to be altruistic while on work hour time, you will make for a very happy staff. They will be motivated by the fact that they are fulfilling a wish that is within their heart to help others, but that they don't have to try and find a way to fit into their already ridiculously busy schedule outside work. That's a major win-win-win. Every Smiles Change Lives patient your staff helps wins, your office wins through the many ways we have already laid out, and your employees win. They will gain all the benefits that come from volunteering and being altruistic.

When your office takes up the mission of working with Smiles Change Lives, you are giving your team a chance to be a part of something bigger. It's something important beyond just taking care of the regular patients who come day in and day out. While we love those patients and are grateful for every one of them, we also love it when we get the chance to truly help someone who wouldn't otherwise be able to get the help. When we help a child through the program, we know we made a big difference in someone's life. Being able to help better someone's life who may not have otherwise had the opportunity is hugely gratifying. Altruism, by definition, is when we act out of concern for another person's well-being. Every time we help a child through the Smiles Change Lives

SMILES CHANGE LIVES : THE SMART ORTHODONTIST'S GUIDE TO GROWING A PURPOSE-DRIVEN PRACTICE

program, that's exactly what we are doing. We know we have the skills and ability to help change their life. We know how important it is to have straight teeth and the impact it can have on their entire life. We have concern for these children and interest in their well-being. We want the best for them to go into life feeling they have a fair shot. The best thing we can share with them is our time and abilities, and that's just what we do.

Engaged Employees

Are you still convinced that your office is too busy to take on helping some kids through the Smiles Change Lives program? Let me give you a few more nuggets to consider then, which may have you thinking otherwise. You may or may not be aware of this but there is a good chance that some of your team members are, well, not at all engaged. They go through the motions, sure, and they get the job done. But they are not engaged, and in fact, some are bored stiff. They clock watch and can't wait to hit the door so they can do something more meaningful and engaging.

In the last chapter, I told you about how Gallup did a whole report on employee engagement. It's such important information to your office that I want to mention it again. They found, "a highly engaged workforce means the difference between a company that outperforms its competitors and one that fails to grow." That's huge. If you don't have a team of employees who are engaged in what they are doing, it is more than likely going to keep your practice from doing better than your competition and it will keep you from growing. Here's something that's even scarier. In that report, they found that 87% of employees around the world are not engaged and that most companies are not even aware of it.

How can it be that you can have a workforce that is not engaged? Simply because you are not looking for it and don't pay close enough attention in order to spot it. Their science is based on 30 years of research and was conducted looking at 30 million employees. If you recall from the last chapter, they further report that companies that have a highly engaged workforce end up outperforming their peers by 147% in earnings per share. Being engaged is good for the employer, and it's good for the employees.

In July 2017, Fortune reported that the average worker in the country spends one full day of their week doing things other than work. That's what all the extras added up to, an entire day per week that is being wasted.

One of the most interesting realizations from this data is that we all feel so busy throughout the week and never seem to "have time" to get everything done.

Their report also found that the average employee spends 56 minutes per day using their cellphone at work, for non-work activities. That's a lot of time that could be used to support the community, and in turn your office would be getting back from that participation.

It doesn't stop there. The same article went on to say that the average employee spends around 3.5 hours per week attending to personal tasks while on the job. These tasks consist of such things as running errands and making personal phone calls. Those offices that have younger workers on their team will experience even more wasted time, because the research shows that employees between the ages of 18-34 end up spending around 70 minutes per day on their mobile phone while on the job and 48 minutes on average taking care of personal tasks. The younger employees rack up around 10 hours per week of time on the job that is not being used for anything to do with their job.

Trust me when I say that I'm not busting your chops on this stuff simply to make you feel inadequate and like you haven't noticed how your team is wasting time. I'm not doing that at all. Nor am I bringing this to your attention to get your employees in trouble. You may even say that this doesn't represent you and your team, that you know your team is not wasting time like this. To that, I would say that unless you have taken the time to really pay attention to it and address it, and engage them more, it likely is happening right under your nose.

But all is not lost. It's never too late to turn it around.

Through my orthodontic consulting work around the country, I have seen many practices that have offices where the employees are not engaged and are wasting precious hours per day. It's not your fault if you didn't notice it before, because you most likely didn't even know to look for it. But now that you are aware of it, you can make changes. Those changes will be huge for your practice. Those hours you save per day can be used for the community support.

You do have the time to help support a program like Smiles Change Lives. I just helped you see the vision and benefits, now you just need to help your team do the same. Nearly everyone wants to help others, and they are fortunate enough to work for someone who is going to give them the opportunity to do it while on the job. You can't beat that.

CHAPTER 6

ABUNDANCE VERSUS SCARCITY

"Remember, no more effort is required to aim high in life, to demand abundance and prosperity than is required to accept misery and poverty." – Napoleon Hill

There's an epidemic that most of the entrepreneurs I have come across suffer from. It's not even limited to entrepreneurs either, it's a problem that is seen across nearly all industries and in all levels of positions within them. What is it? It's the scarcity mindset, and it's a problem that is crippling millions of people. The scarcity mindset keeps most people from ever reaching their true potential. It's what holds most orthodontic practices back, and there's a good chance that you suffer from it, too.

Before you start feeling guilty about having a scarcity mindset, let me first fill you in on what it is and why it's such a problem. It's also important for you to realize that it is not your fault you have this mindset. It's truly not, at least up until the point that someone, such as myself, brings the concept to your attention. Once you learn about it, if you still have a scarcity mindset then it is your fault, because you are deciding to be that way, knowing what it can and will keep you from achieving. But up until the point that someone brings it to your attention and shows you a better way, you simply didn't know, so it's not your fault.

In this chapter, I'm going to challenge you to start thinking big. I'm going to bring the ideas of abundance and scarcity to your attention and help you identify them in your own way of thinking. After reading this chapter, you should have a whole new outlook on the concept and hopefully put it into action to change the rest of your life. Trust me when I say that it's that powerful.

Abundance and scarcity come down to one thing. Your mindset. It's all in how you look at the world, and it makes an amazing difference. Not just in you and what you can accomplish, but also in your staff. The mindset of your employees makes a world of difference to your practice's success.

Living in Abundance

Think about the last time your employees were able to give someone a $5,000 - $6,000 gift. My treatment coordinators, administrative employees and clinical team get to perform this magical act every single day. When a Smiles Change Lives patient comes to our practice and my team learns the power and appreciation from giving such a powerful gift, they are more likely to see the world with abundance.

Employees with an abundant mindset are happier at work. They are more likely to be generous with those around them. They treat their coworkers with more respect. They are nicer to their patients. And, they feel confident in what they do and the value in the service they provide. Because they are accustomed to giving $5,000 and $6,000 gifts to patients who really need help, they aren't shy about asking for money from those who can pay.

I've witnessed the generosity spill over into their personal lives. In our monthly employee newsletter, I see more reports and stories of employees donating their time and money to charitable causes and doing bigger and more exciting things in their lives, learning new skills, reading more books – all because they see the world with abundance and not from a viewpoint of scarcity. It's something that most of us have been taught since we could walk. We have been conditioned to see the world as a place of scarcity and to fear the idea that there is abundance.

Think about your childhood conditioning. Most of us were taught things like, "money is hard earned" or, "money doesn't grow on trees." I was taught to always finish my food because, "some kid in some poor country is starving." This is bad advice that parents give without thinking. By teaching your child that money and food are scarce, you teach him or her to think with a limited mindset. I'll never forget the day I learned from a very successful mentor who grew up dirt poor why he always leaves a little bite of steak on his plate at a fancy restaurant. "I do it to remind myself that this is an abundant world," he said, "That cow was already born, bred, butchered and sitting in this restaurant's refrigerator whether I came here tonight and ordered the steak or not. My decision to leave a little bit on the plate has no impact on some child in a third world country, but my mindset and my ability to support my company, my clients, my employees and all of the stakeholders and shareholders in my firm is very much impacted by my ability to see the world with abundance." He continued, "Think of the farmers and laborers who raised that cow and the butcher and the truck driver who brought it to the restaurant and the chef and the line cooks and the waiter and bus boy who will all benefit as a result of this meal tonight." When you think like this extremely successful entrepreneur, it's almost impossible to see the world as anything other than extremely abundant. It's hard to have anyone around you who doesn't thrive.

Therefore, I openly donate my time, talent, money and energy to Smiles Change Lives. Because it helps everyone around me thrive and stay focused on a vision of the world that is extremely abundant.

Changing Your Mind

If you want your orthodontic practice to succeed, you must start by changing your mindset. You'll never outperform your self-image and you'll never reach a high level of success by thinking small. There is no room for scarcity thinking. You must change the thoughts that dominate your mind from those of lack and scarcity to plenty and abundance.

Think Positive!

I highly recommend picking up the book "The Magic of Thinking Big" by Dr. David Schwartz. Reading the book and applying the concepts will be nothing short of life changing for you and your staff. While you are at it, pick up a copy for everyone in your office. Give them each the assignment of reading it, so that everyone on your team is on the same page, and they will all be thinking big. Once they read the book, they will be looking at the world in terms of abundance, rather than scarcity. Like you, there's a good chance that nobody has ever taken the time to share the information with them. You will be doing them a huge favor by essentially giving them a key to their successful future.

In the book, there's a quote that says, "Those who believe they can move mountains, do. Those who believe they can't, cannot. Belief triggers the power to do."

Think about that for a moment. What that comes down to is that what we believe we can do is what we end up doing. If you or your team believes that your office is too busy to take on a Smiles Change Lives patient, then guess what? You'll be unlikely to welcome Smiles Change Lives patients and their referrals to your practice. Your mindset has already defeated you, and you will not be successful in the endeavor. On the other hand, if you believe you can fit in taking on three or four more patients, then you will do so, and you will be successful at it. Our mindset is amazingly powerful when it comes to what we will achieve in life.

As Schwartz points out, believing in success is the one basic, essential ingredient of successful people. Those who don't believe in success, well, they never find it. But those who do believe in success find it, and they often find it in a big way. Their mindset of abundance is the driving force to being wildly successful. Successful people don't allow the idea of scarcity or a negative mindset to hold them back. They realize how important and powerful thinking big is to their future and to their success.

Here's something highly important to remember too: If you have doubt in your mind, then you don't have a mindset for success. That little inkling of doubt will indeed hold you back. You will be one of the many people who don't achieve your goals, don't become the success you want to become, and you will have an excuse. You will say that you had your doubts about it from the start or that you gave it a try, but you still didn't think that it would work.

The world is filled with people who tried something without having the mindset that it would help them to be successful.

If you go forward with trying something, yet your mindset is still focused on scarcity and that you doubt it will work, guess what will happen? It won't work, and you won't succeed. If you have a negative mindset yet keep moving forward to "give it a shot," you are likely just wasting your time. When your mind doesn't believe something or has doubts, it will attract all the silly reasons it can think of to support your ideas about scarcity. On the other hand, when you focus on abundance and believe that something will work, you will attract all the reasons that it will work, and you will be a success.

Which do you want to attract in your quest to become highly successful? Do you want to attract all the thoughts that will help you not succeed, or do you want to attract those thoughts and ideas that will help you achieve your goals? Which do you think your team would rather be attracting? You hold the key to which type of reasons and ideas you will attract. It's all a matter of whether you have a mindset of abundance or scarcity.

One of the most important quotes you can ever hear in life is one by Schwartz, who said "A person is a product of his own thoughts."

Think about that. Everything you are today, you are because of your thoughts. You thought everything into being. Your attitude and ideas, which are all part of your mindset, lead you right to where and who you are today in your life.

But it doesn't stop there. You still need to use your mind to determine the next stage, the next chapter, and what course you will take going forward. You are the product of your own thoughts, just as everyone on your team is the product of their own thoughts. If you don't like something, change it by changing the way you think. If you want more out of life, if you want to take your practice to the next level, if you want to do something more meaningful, no matter what it is, it all starts with your own thoughts. Did you ever stop to realize that you and what you think are so powerful?

Here's something you can quickly do to gauge your mindset and its relation to your level of success. Take out a sheet of paper and write the names of three people you have known for a while who have become

THOSE WHO BELIEVE THEY CAN
MOVE MOUNTAINS, DO. THOSE WHO
BELIEVE THEY CAN'T, CANNOT.
BELIEF TRIGGERS THE POWER TO DO.

more successful than you are. Then, ask yourself what it is that each of those three people have that you don't have. Are they smarter or better educated? Do they have better habits than you do? Why do you think it is that they have all surpassed you in terms of success? The answer to this usually comes down to one thing. You probably guessed it after reading through this chapter too. It's mindset. Those who believe they will succeed and see the world in which they live as having abundance tend to become far more successful. Those who see the world as having scarcity and believe that only some people succeed will most likely never reach their full potential. They will, on the other hand, have an arm's length list of excuses of all the things that have kept them from being successful. Their mind has helped them to generate that list so that it continues to support their position and lack of mindset.

Not only can you and your team do better than that, but you must if you want to be highly successful. And I have a sneaking suspicion that you do want to be highly successful. We all do. It's in our nature to want to succeed, but it's not in our nature to have the ambition or mindset to help us make it happen. The good news is that now that you are aware of this, you can make the necessary adjustment to change the way you think so you can harness the power of thinking in abundance and in thinking big.

Changing Your Mindset

At this point, I hope I have convinced you that your mindset is going to make all the difference in how far you go in life. You are probably wondering how you change your mindset to one that has you winning at life. That's a great question and it's one that many people before you have pondered and found the answers to. Not only will this information help you to change your mindset, but share it with your team, and it will have a profound impact on them as well. Your practice will have nowhere to go but up when everyone on your team shares the same mindset, one of abundance.

Some experts claim that we have somewhere between 50,000-70,000 thoughts per day. Your mind is constantly switching to different thoughts, almost like someone is holding a television remote control and hitting the button over and over to change it. The problem with having so many thoughts per day is that psychologists believe around 70% of them are negative. Most thoughts you are having during the day are focusing on scarcity or lack. Your mind is constantly coming up with excuses, fabricating scare tactics, and giving you reasons to not do something.

That's difficult to get past, I get it. But let me remind you that you have control over your mind. If you are having thousands of negative thoughts per day, it's because that's what you are attracting. This is something that you can control. It is within your power to change this thought pattern, and in doing so, it changes your life. Working with Smiles Change Lives has been just one important way that we have done this in our practice. When we focus on abundance and match that up with altruism, you have a winning combination that is going to take you straight to the top.

The way you think now is how you have been most likely thinking for decades. It's time to change that in yourself and help your staff to make the same change. It's the only way your practice is ever going to be highly successful. The great thing here is that you can change the way you think. It may take some effort, but you absolutely can turn it around.

For starters, you need to make the decision that you are going to change the way you think. You will no longer focus on scarcity, but instead focus on abundance. You must replace negative thoughts with positive ones and focus on success. Don't let thoughts of failure rule your mind. If one does creep in, recognize that it's there, and immediately change the thought to be one of abundance. Whatever life throws at you, begin responding with the attitude that you will win, you will succeed, and you will come out ahead. When a great opportunity comes your way, don't come up with a list of excuses as to why it won't work or why you can't do it. Embrace the opportunity, and go into it with a success-driven mindset that will help you win.

Next, you must believe in yourself, and don't settle for less than the best. Remember the exercise we did where you wrote the three names down of those who have surpassed you in terms of success? If you recall, these people are not somehow better than you are. They are not smarter or better educated either. The only difference between you and them is attitude. They believe in themselves and have an amazing amount of self-confidence, while your beliefs about yourself continue to hold you back.

Finally, you want to set big goals. Forget the little ones that are largely meaningless. You have only been setting these little goals because you were lacking the confidence and mindset to think bigger. Now that you know the importance of thinking big and how to have the right mindset to do it, you should settle for nothing less. Thinking big is how you achieve big. You can't achieve big results with small thinking and small goals. It doesn't work like that. If you want to reach the big goals, you must think big.

Moving Forward, Big Thoughts

You are probably wondering about now what this whole mindset thing has to do with Smiles Change Lives. Fair enough. The reason I bring up the importance of your mindset and that of your team is because many people immediately want to think negatively. Many orthodontists I've spoken to about this program immediately give the hand wave and say they are too busy. They don't see at all how it can play a role in helping their staff to become more engaged or for their office to become far more successful.

"What the mind can conceive and believe, it can achieve."
– Napoleon Hill

I'm a firm believer that whether you have a mind that is focused on scarcity or abundance, it has a major connection to your level of success. I am also a firm believer in the Smiles Change Lives program and all that it can do to not only help people who need our services but also come back to help your practice.

The Smiles Change Lives program doesn't just change the life of the person who is receiving the orthodontic treatment. That's the beauty of this program. The lives that are changed reach far beyond the dental chair, touching everyone in your office and those in your community. With the right mindset you can use this program, as I have done, to help take your practice to the next level. You can use it to help you get more referrals that you will know what to do with, as well as use it to help engage your staff and get them feeling great about what they do.

The program is so powerful, which is why it's called Smiles Change Lives to begin with. It changes lives, starting with yours. It starts with the orthodontist who sees the beauty and opportunity in the program, embraces it, and lets it take them right to the top.

CHAPTER 7

A HIGHER SENSE OF PURPOSE

"Study the lives of successful people and you'll discover this: all the excuses made by the mediocre fellow could be but aren't made by the successful person."
– David J. Schwartz

When was the last time you took a good look at your team of employees? Have you thought about your turnover rate and what that could mean for your practice? According to the Bureau of Labor Statistics, the median number of years that someone has been with their current employer is only 4.2 years. That's not a long time, which leads me to the next question, which is - why is that? Why are people staying with their employer for around 4 years before feeling that it's time to move on to what they probably feel are greener pastures?

Most orthodontists don't give much thought to their team or at least as much thought as they should. They hire some people who seem good from their resumes and from the interview, and then things are put on autopilot for a while. Well, a lot happens during the time that it's all on autopilot. What I've found through consulting with orthodontists around the world is that they often lose their best employees within a couple of years. And as luck would have it, they tend to retain some of the not-so-great employees. That's probably because those people, well, they lack the initiative and drive to seek something else. Good for them that they still have a job, but not good for your office if you have an employee who doesn't love being there and is only sticking around because they don't have the initiative to seek another position.

Most orthodontists don't know exactly what it is that makes people on their team stay or go. Some will throw more money toward the person they want to keep, assuming it's all about a paycheck. But that's not what the research shows, and the more you know about what motivates your employees, the more successful your practice can become. You can use that information, like one more tool in your toolbox, to help retain your best employees and help motivate them to give their all when they're on the job.

More than Money

Think about it. If you did your job and hired talented employees, they could almost certainly leave your office and go work somewhere else tomorrow. So, why do they come to work for you? Is it for a paycheck, as so many orthodontists believe? Is it for the retirement plan and health insurance? If you think your employees show up in your parking lot each Monday morning and walk through your doors because of the tangible benefits alone, you are not only fooling yourself, but you're also in opposition to the research.

Dr. Barry Schwartz and his team of researchers interviewed over 30,000 employees at successful organizations and asked them when they felt like they were contributing the most to their job and when they were the happiest. It was never associated with a financial incentive, pay raise or any other monetary measurement. Employees felt the most rewarded, valued and happiest in their work when they were attached to a higher sense of purpose, had the ability to master something new, and were given more autonomy in how they produced results.

If you and your team haven't had a conversation about the higher sense of purpose you bring into your marketplace and into the universe, now is the time to do so. As an orthodontist, I understand how much you help patients with poor occlusion, breathing and airway problems, jaw joint pain, teasing or embarrassment about their smiles, etc. But I think there is a higher sense of purpose in helping more people achieve healthy, confident smiles so they can live their best life and show up to their first date or first job interview with confidence.

That is one of the things I absolutely love about working with Smiles Change Lives. Yes, my office helps many people throughout the week. But they are typically people who have the means to afford that life-changing treatment. It's when we help the Smiles Change Lives patients that we are truly doing something that is bigger than ourselves. We are engaging in a true sense of higher purpose, and we are engaged in supporting those in need on a meaningful level.

The treatment we provide to a Smiles Change Lives patient is truly life changing, and it's something that they most likely would not have been able to get without our assistance. I have gone into detail explaining how being a part of this great program benefits our office, and it absolutely does. It's been a cornerstone to helping to create a highly successful practice. But it doesn't stop there because the real reward is the personal feelings we get in response to every patient we provide treatment to. When we see the difference in that person's life that we have made, it in turn makes a difference in our lives.

A Problem We Face

When I say that helping a Smiles Change Lives patient is life changing for that person, I truly mean it. If you are familiar with the bullying problem that is being experienced around the country, you can see the connection. The more we can do to help alleviate the bullying problem, the better off we will be. Young people are being bullied at alarming rates, and it's something that we can all help to end.

The facts surrounding bullying are nothing short of disheartening. During the very years that these young people should be having fun and really

enjoying life, they are so often being made to feel miserable by their bullying peers.

When that happens, it often goes on to have detrimental consequences that can last a lifetime. Those younger years, when a child is absorbing everything around them, are crucial to their development and even who they will become as an adult.

According to the Centers for Disease Control and Prevention (CDC), when it comes to bullying in America:

- One out of every three students report that they have been bullied at school, and there are others who say they have experienced cyberbullying (being bullied in an electronic format, such as online).

- The most prevalent years for bullying take place during middle school. The most common types of bullying that people experience during this time are verbal and social bullying.

- They report that bullying remains a prevalent and serious problem in today's schools in America.

- One of the biggest risk factors for being bullied is young people who are perceived to be different from their peers.

Who is it that is most likely to be bullied? Although bullying probably wasn't as common when you were going to school as it is today, think about who it was who got teased back then. If you are like most of us, you probably saw the student with the malocclusion who commonly got teased. Those kids were easy targets for those who were looking for someone to tease. They stood out, they looked a bit different, and the bullies found it easy to get others in the classroom or on the playground to go ahead and join in or laugh about their teeth.

The effects of bullying cannot be overstated. They can help to shape these young people, change them, and help determine who they will be as adults. A child who is being bullied is less likely to want to engage in school functions, will be less outgoing, will shy away from interacting with people, and may become withdrawn and depressed. The CDC reports that kids who are bullied experience negative physical, social, and mental health issues.

Being bullied has also been linked to having negative effects on their mental health, substance abuse, and suicide. Kids who are bullied tend to experience more depression, anxiety, sadness, loneliness, health problems and complaints, and they tend to have decreased academic achievement. Victims of bullying, the research shows, are more likely to skip, miss, and drop out of school, as well as have a lower grade point average.

As if that information isn't enough to persuade you to want to change the world, one mouth at a time, through the Smiles Change Lives program, consider these research study findings:

- In the July 2017 issue of the Journal of Pediatric Dentistry, researchers shared their findings from a study that looked at suspected cases of abuse and neglect that had been submitted by health providers (including dentists). The information has been collected across all 50 states. They reported that "oral health issues can be associated with bullying and are commonly seen in human trafficking victims."

- In the December 2016 issue of the Journal of the Irish Dental Association, they reported that "orthodontic treatment can have a positive impact on the psychosocial well-being of patients who are bullied about dentofacial features." They shared information about a student who was being badly bullied. They provided early treatment to correct the problem, with the treatment including orthodontic alignment of the arches, early orthognathic bimaxillary surgery and post-surgical orthodontics to detail the occlusion. The outcome? They report that there was a dramatic improvement in the patient's self-esteem.

- In the January 2014 issue of the European Journal of Dentistry, the researchers report that oral aesthetics can severely affect a child's quality of life and can cause physical, social, and psychological impairment. They also report that children with aesthetic-related issues are targets for bullies. They advised that providing an adequate aesthetic dental treatment is an important step in their rehabilitation when it is the source of the child being bullied. They report that after the dental treatments, there was a significant improvement in self-esteem, self-confidence, socialization, and academic performance.

IF YOU AND YOUR TEAM HAVEN'T HAD A CONVERSATION ABOUT THE HIGHER SENSE OF PURPOSE YOU BRING INTO YOUR MARKETPLACE AND INTO THE UNIVERSE, NOW IS THE TIME TO DO SO.

- While most of us would love to believe that the impact of bullying is done once kids finish high school, that's just not the case. In the January 2019 issue of the Journal of American College Health, the authors reported that time and support does not heal all bullying wounds. They found that mental health correlates to past bullying in college students. They evaluated if being bullied in middle and high school was associated with being depressed, anxious, and having post-traumatic stress disorder in college. They concluded that bullying in middle and high school was associated with more problems during college, and that the college students who had been bullied needed counseling in order to reduce the symptoms.

This is just a sampling of the peer-reviewed research that is out there on the impact that bullying has on our youth. Unfortunately, there's a lot more where these came from. The research on the impact of bullying goes on and on. And it's not pretty. Study after study lays out the dangerous problem that we have in this nation, not just in terms of the bullying taking place to begin with, but in the long-term and lasting effects that it has.

Bullying is no joke. It's something that can destroy lives. The good news is that as an orthodontist, you are in the position to help end it. You can help improve lives for the better. It's not just while kids are in middle and high school, but the treatment you provide to a child in the Smiles Change Lives program will have a long-term impact. I can't reiterate enough how the treatment you provide through this program is truly life changing.

Imagine you get a patient who is referred to you through the Smiles Change Lives program. This patient has a noticeable misalignment. It's one that is holding them back; it's keeping this child from participating more in school. It makes the child not want to try out for the school play. It makes the child too embarrassed to give their report on world

history in front of the classroom so he or she skips doing the assignment and doesn't show up to school on the day they are supposed to give the report. By high school, the child can barely look people in the eye, because he or she has become used to being teased. They have spent so much time being the butt end of people's jokes and bullying that they no longer have the desire to engage with peers. They stick to themselves, shy away from others, and feel they are not worthy of having friends, being a part of the team, or going out on dates.

By this time, the student's self-esteem has sunk so low that there could be severe consequences that come as a result. Perhaps they become depressed, turn to suicide, or they decide to numb the pain and shut the bullying voices up by taking drugs or drinking alcohol. Who knows where this student will be once he graduates, if he or she graduates, and what impact it will have going into the adult years. These are very important years, when self-esteem is desperately needed in order to apply for and maintain a job, ask people out on dates, assert yourself and find your place in this world.

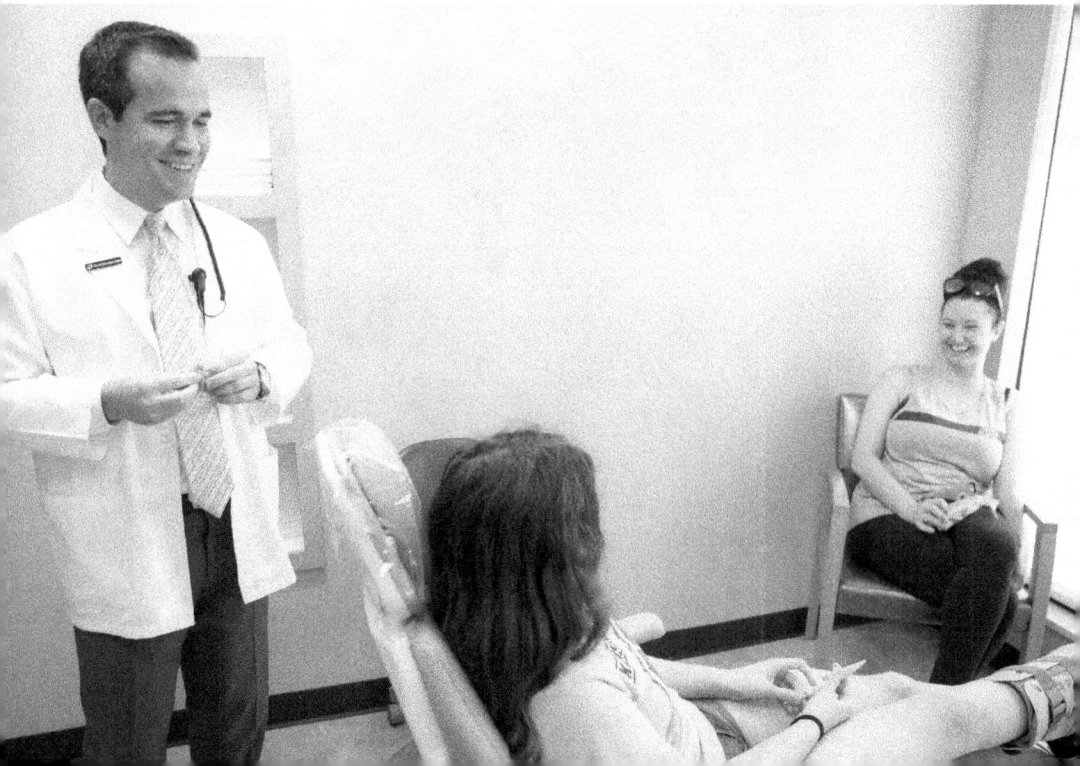

You can imagine how life is going to go for most of those students who were bullied due to their teeth, especially if they were never fixed. You and I both know that it takes money to fix teeth. Yet the impact of having them fixed is tremendous. Not everyone can afford it, so some people will have no choice but to go through their middle and high school years with the problem, absorbing the bullying, and all that it entails. They have no other choice at that point. We can all close our eyes to the fact that this is happening, or we can use our skills to try and do something about it. For my practice, I choose the latter, and it has made all the difference.

As an orthodontist, you have an amazing ability that can help people in a profound way. It's such an important contribution that we tend to take for granted as we go about providing treatment day in and day out.

But make no mistake, the work we are doing is helping to make for a better world, because it helps to create happier, better-adjusted people. Everyone we help goes out into the world a better version of themselves, and I'm not just talking esthetically. They are better mentally, too, and people who are better mentally will be better-adjusted citizens who help to create a better world.

Practice with a Purpose

Research published in the March 2018 journal, Frontiers in Psychology, looked at the idea of meaningful work. They explain that humans are hardwired to seek meaning, and that when there is a lack of meaning, it is associated with such things as depression, mortality, and even suicidal ideation. Don't get me wrong, I'm not saying that if you don't help patients through Smiles Change Lives that your staff will not have meaning and will go on to become suicidal or depressed. That's not at all what I'm saying. But I do think it's important for you to know how important meaningful work is, and that you absolutely do have the ability to help give your employees the gift of purpose through their work. Perhaps they don't even realize that sense of purpose is missing at this point, but there will come a day when they do. Whether they do or not, you can interject their life with a sense of purpose and give more meaning to their work.

The researchers in the article share that finding meaning is about connecting. They report that "meanings are the expected relationships and associations that human beings see in their world. In this sense meanings are constructed; they are something we impose upon the world." Many people are looking for fulfillment within their jobs; and they are longing for a way to make a connection. Further, they report that meaningfulness is what guides, directs, and gives value to what it is that we are doing.

One of the areas the researchers in this study delve into is that of people having a broader purpose, which is the idea that the work they are doing must contribute to a "greater good." It's about the idea that workers are being a part of something bigger and greater than themselves. It's about making a valuable contribution to society. The researchers back up what I've said many times over, which is that people don't find their salary to be what makes work purposeful. Rather, they report that people find meaningful work when they participate in a larger system of shared values, rather than just their own personal interests.

I'm going to go out on a limb here and say that you have probably never considered your employees having a sense of higher purpose or a connection to the greater good. I say this because that's the norm. I have worked in consulting enough orthodontists around the world to know that it's something that is almost never thought of. Rather, their time is spent focusing on the daily tasks of the position and keeping the office running. But it's so much more valuable than that.

You want your practice to work like a well-oiled machine. You want your office to grow and become more successful than you could ever imagine.

But, what if I told you that you have been looking at the wrong areas to focus on to help make that happen? Would you believe me and take my word for it? Would you give it shot to see if I was on to something? After all, you literally have nothing to lose but a little bit of your office's time, considering Smiles Change Lives provides the necessary hardware for providing treatment to patients.

Some people would say that I'm the biggest cheerleader for the Smiles Change Lives program. And maybe they are right. I don't know how loud others are cheering. But what I do know is that it is a program that, as its name says, changes lives.

Once you take the leap and decide to start working with the Smiles Change Lives program, you then need to have a meeting with your staff. Get them excited about what they are contributing towards and help them see the important work that they will be a part of, and the amazing difference in young people's lives they will be helping to create. Then, put it all into action and watch the magic happen.

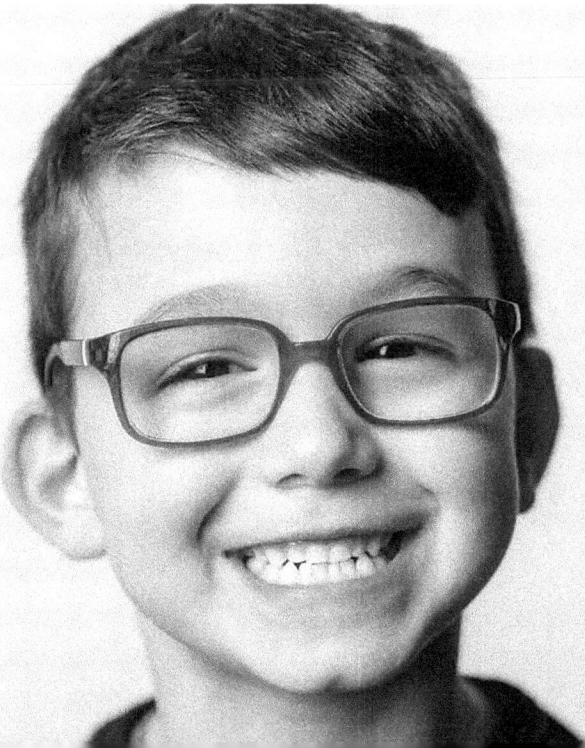

CHAPTER 8

ATTRACT
THE BEST
EMPLOYEES

"Teamwork is the ability to work together toward a common vision. The ability to direct individual accomplishments toward organizational objectives. It is the fuel that allows common people to attain uncommon results." — Andrew Carnegie

When it comes down to it, it doesn't matter if you are the best damn orthodontist on the planet if you are not surrounded by the right people. Your team will either help make, or help break, you and your efforts. You can only do so much so you must have a team in your office that is made up of the best people who will share in and carry out your vision. Are you doing all you can do to help make that happen?

Most orthodontists need to fill positions, so they grab the best candidate that applies at that time. They may not even be thrilled with the pool they have to choose from, but they make their selection and hope for the best. But hoping for the best isn't good enough and will never help your practice to be the success you want and need it to be. Not only can you do better than this, but you must do better than this. Your practice weighs in the balance, and the difference between your office being wildly successful, being mediocre, and being a failure largely comes down to the team you have working alongside you.

The importance of your team and the difference they make to your office's success cannot be overstated. The time you spend on ensuring that you are attracting and retaining the best employees possible will pay off handsomely. It's the most important thing you can do for your practice.

While we've looked at employee engagement and your employees having a higher sense of purpose in prior chapters, in this one I want to emphasize the importance of attracting high-quality employees. I'll share with you some of my experience in this area, what I have seen by consulting other orthodontists, what some of the research shows, and finally, what some of the most successful companies out there are doing to attract the best employees.

There's an important question I have new coaching clients ask their employees anonymously. You might want to try it yourself. You can set up a free account on SurveyMonkey and ask your employees this one question: **"Knowing what you know now, would you recommend a friend or family member come work at this practice? Yes or no."** If more than a few employees in your practice say "no," you have a major problem on your hands.

It's painful for me to admit, but when I used to treat only one or two Smiles Change Lives kids per year, I had a major problem with my employees and the answer to this question. Paying them well and treating them nicely wasn't enough to get them to stay. In my offices we work hard, and we make a lot of money, but that isn't enough to keep people around. When I opened my mind to a world of abundance and helped my employees do the same, the answer to this question changed dramatically. Ask the question, review the results, and contemplate the changes you need to make.

By the time you finish this chapter, you will be taking a hard look at your current team and how your office is run, and you will either pat yourself on the back for a job well done, or you will begin to see where things have fallen short. Don't despair. That's where progress begins, because you can, at that point, start making changes that will lead to amazing benefits for your practice.

What Employees Want

As employers, we know what we want from our employees. We give them the list of duties when they get hired. If they are lucky, they will work at an orthodontic office that gives them the training they need to do the job. If they are even luckier yet, they will receive some ongoing training, which will help to advance their skills and make them an even more valuable team player. But skills aside, there's something even more valuable to your office. That is attitude.

We can train our team members to do the tasks that we want done. We can teach them how we want them done and have them follow a list, line by line, to ensure that everything is carried out just so. But we can't make them have a positive attitude. Sure, I know what you are thinking. They can put on a smile and be courteous. Yet anyone who comes into your office can see and feel that it's not authentic. People have an energy about them, and if they are happy and enjoy what they are doing, it shows, and those around them feel it. You can't make someone have that kind of attitude. That comes from within, and it comes from the feeling of being grateful to be where they are, and that they are making a difference.

So, we know what we want from employees, or at least, we should. My bet is that you know what types of tasks you want your employees to carry out, but then it stops there. You don't think about much beyond

that. But what do they want out of a job? Are we merely a paycheck to them? Are we just a source of benefits for their family? Let's look at some of the things that employees want.

Gallup has conducted extensive research on the issue of what employees want and why top employees leave a company. The results of their study may surprise you and they may motivate you to see how important it is to make some changes in your office. For starters, they issued a paper regarding why the best employees are leaving their jobs. Now, as discussed in a prior chapter, one of the most common reasons across the board that employees leave a company is that they are not engaged. Companies tend to lose their least engaged employees most often. But beyond that, they wanted to know why the top employees leave companies.

You don't want to lose your most talented employees because they are worth gold to your practice. Perhaps you didn't realize that. Maybe you live by the notion that some people do, which is that "everyone is replaceable." Well, you may be able to replace someone, as in have a physical body come into their position, but that doesn't mean you will replace their talent level, dedication to the field, passion for what your mission is, and so on. That's a whole other animal in trying to replace all of that, so it's a good idea to sit up and take notice of why top employees tend to leave.

What Gallup found from their research is that your top employees are leaving, well, for the same exact reason that your other employees leave. It primarily comes down to a lack of engagement. It's not because they want a raise or better benefits. It's not because they want a new title or to move into a different position. It's simply because they are not engaged. How do you change that? Well, you can do that by engaging them in a mission that supports a higher purpose. Being a part of the Smiles Change Lives program does exactly that.

In the same report, they advised that management should keep this formula in mind:

Talent x Engagement x Tenure = High Performance

First, you need to hire the best talent. Therefore, it is important to have a practice that attracts the best employees. If you run an ad that you are hiring for a position, but word on the street is that your place isn't the best to work for, then do you think you will ever have the best talent applying for the job? Of course not. But if your office has a great reputation as an incredible place to work, a place where you can not only earn a good paycheck, but you can be a part of something meaningful, then you will indeed attract applications from the best talent out there.

Once you have the talent in place, the next piece is engagement. The engagement is what gives the person the drive to come back into your office week after week and keep doing what they do. Their passion for what they do drives them and keeps them invested in it every step of the way. Add talent and engagement together, and you will have tenure. Gallup reports that having tenure without having talent and engagement has a very small impact on performance. But, and this is the important part, when you have high talent and engagement, the tenure will pay off, and your employees will become masters at their craft. That's a big boost to your practice.

PERFORMANCE

If you can keep your top employees, it's going to pay off well over the years. According to the Gallup figures, when you have an employee who has talent, is engaged, and has been with your company for at least 10 years, they will perform 18% higher than the average employee and a whopping 35% higher than workers who lack those important elements.

About this time, you are looking around at your staff and thinking about who fits the bill and who doesn't. Good.

Gallup also reports that your employees are more likely to be led by emotion. This is more influential to them than reason. Giving someone a pay increase to keep them from leaving, for example, is based on reason. But giving employees something to believe in and be a part of that is truly making a difference in the world, well, that's based on emotion. That will have much more meaning to them and will help to enrich their lives.

Furthermore, 36% of employees say the company's reputation is "very important" to them when considering where to take a job. The company's reputation is even more important to female employees and baby boomers. This is another perk when it comes to being a part of the Smiles Change Lives program. Being a part of the program helps to give your office a wonderful reputation, and well deserved, because of the great work you are doing in helping to change lives, one smile at a time.

When we send out our employee newsletter and talk about the wins in the practice at team meetings, every single time, someone shares a story about one of our Smiles Change Lives patients. They are so grateful and appreciative for the work we do for them and they are so kind and positive about the orthodontic experience that it's hard for your employees not to fall in love with the charitable work they will do for Smiles Change Lives.

It's this higher sense of purpose and new outlook on life that you provide for them as their leader that will keep them coming back and referring their friends and family to work in your office.

Creating Your Environment

I want to stress here how important it is that you manage your environment and that in doing so, you shoot for the stars. When you have ideas that you think can make your practice better, more effective, and ultimately more profitable, you will always have some who feel otherwise. It's in some people's nature to automatically be negative and just want to downplay what you say. Or perhaps they may even try to talk you out of it. They purposely try to sabotage your enthusiasm for the idea, or if they are really a drag, they may try to sabotage the plan itself. You can't allow this to happen.

In the book I mentioned in a previous chapter (which I highly recommend reading), "The Magic of Thinking Big," David J. Schwartz explains to readers how important it is that you create your environment. If you want to succeed and have a highly successful practice, then you and you and alone need to create the conditions for that to happen. You are responsible for your environment. You are going to have some negative people in your office who may not want to engage in the Smiles Change Lives program or anything that you want to do to take your practice to the next level. These "Negative Nancy's", or as Schwartz refers to them, "negators," are everywhere. But it's important that you don't let them hold you back.

Schwartz explains how these negators, or negative-thinking people, will destroy your plan to think yourself to success. They are people who are just about everywhere, and they enjoy holding people back from progress. His advice, which I agree with, is to develop a defense against people who want to convince you that you can't do it. Only accept

negative advice as a challenge to prove that you can do something. Negative opinions can be poison, and you certainly don't need that when you are trying to have a successful and meaningful practice.

Another important thing he warns of when creating your own environment are the pitfalls that are within your office. Every group has at least one person who will secretly want to stand in your way and keep you from reaching your goals. Don't let negative thinkers drive the business, make the decisions, bring you down, or cast a shadow over your plans and ideas. Sometimes people are negative because they themselves can't achieve or reach goals, so they take those feelings and project them onto others. At other times, you may find people who are jealous and want to hold you back. Still others may just be negative because that's the kind of person they are. They can't see the good or benefits because they are blocking the light with their own body.

Just as you watch your diet, take care of your teeth and keep your car looking great, you want to manage your environment. Strive to be conscious of what your environment is like and whether it is how you want it to be. If not, make changes so that it is supportive of your goals and won't hold you back. Make sure that your environment works for you, rather than you always feeling like you are in opposition to it. It's also important to get advice from people who are successful. Why would you take advice from people who are not successful and haven't achieved their own goals? How could they possibly provide you with the motivation you need?

Your team is part of your environment. As mentioned, they can help make your practice a raving success and the office the community loves or they can help make your practice a nearly non-existent option that the community loathes. The choice is all yours, and it all comes down to attracting the best employees. People want to feel they are making a difference in the world and by working with the Smiles Change Lives program you can do just that.

Building Better Teams

To create the best workplace environment and support your team, look at what other successful companies are doing. Sure, you may never aspire to be as big as some of these corporations that I'll mention, but there's no denying that their quest for success is admirable and can most likely be repeated in some form on a smaller scale.

There's always something we can learn from the best. I take every opportunity to study those companies that are highly successful, so that I can see what they did to get there, what they continued to do to stay there, and how they are treating their employees. Their example can be useful in helping you to create your own systems that will help you achieve your growth and success goals.

One of my favorite companies to study is Disney. They are the shining example of not only what success looks like but also an example of how treating their employees well makes a huge difference in that success. Their reputation of treating their guests is second only to their reputation in being a great place to work and one where their cast members are treated exceptionally well. They are fully aware that a great team of cast members is the best way for them to carry out their mission and vision in creating "the happiest place on Earth."

The Disney theme parks in Florida and California get around 68 million visitors per year, and it is estimated that they have around 70,000 cast members who work at their parks and facilities. They often publicly acknowledge that their cast members are the most valuable assets, and they routinely put their money where their mouth is by providing those cast members a wide variety of benefits.

Among those benefits are educational benefits - their cast members receive their full tuition paid for education they obtain at the Disney

THERE IS ALWAYS SOMETHING YOU CAN LEARN FROM THE BEST.

Aspire network schools. They also take care of all costs for books, materials, and the application fees for these courses. These schools provide a variety of degrees and vocational training as well as higher education degrees. They will even provide the cast members with coaches to help with the enrollment process. This is a benefit whose value to their cast members outweighs the price of the tuition greatly as they are receiving the gift of education which can serve them for a lifetime.

Another company which is highly successful and provides a similar educational benefit to their employees is Starbucks. Starbucks pays for 100% of their employees' college tuition when they are earning a full-time bachelor's degree. Considering the rising cost of education, this benefit is a very lucrative benefit to attract quality employees to their organization and it's a strong motivator for retention as well. They have teamed up with Arizona State University to help make it happen, giving employees the opportunity to earn their degrees online if they choose, and there are around 80 different degree programs that employees can select from. That's nothing short of awesome for both Starbucks and their employees.

Besides just the educational benefit, Starbucks is known for treating their employees extremely well in general. Like Disney, they understand that their employees are their most valuable assets. Happy, engaged employees provide better customer service, and there's no doubt that these policies have grown Starbucks in a brand that is a household name with over 60 million customers being served every week.

There is an old adage that states: "People who feel appreciated will always do more than is required." Starbucks would never have reached that level of success without being focused on their employees feeling appreciated and being a great place to work. They strive to make their team members feel like they are part of something bigger than themselves and the return on that investment has been to become a corporate powerhouse.

Both Disney and Starbucks are two examples, among many others, who now pay for college education for their employees, encouraging them to climb up the ranks into higher level positions. It is certain that other companies will begin to see the immense value in doing this for their employees, so there is no doubt that the list of companies offering this benefit will grow soon.

Providing employees with an education is just one example of a great benefit that a company can use to raise their reputation as a great place to work. But, it is just as important to instill a sense of purpose and of being a part of something bigger in your staff as well.

Here's where the Smiles Change Lives program comes in. Participating in the program is a huge benefit to working in your practice that you can't really put a price tag on. It allows your team members to truly make a difference in someone else's life - in this case deserving children who will gain the ability to boost their confidence and self-esteem with a great smile. Raising your revenue per employee and providing them other perks are great, but this type of engagement and monumental change in the life of a young person is one that will deliver your team a great deal of personal fulfillment and satisfaction that will stay with them for years to come.

CHAPTER 9:

THINK
BIG

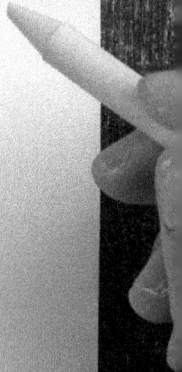

> *"Big thinkers are specialists in creating positive, forward-looking, optimistic pictures in their own minds and in the minds of others." – David J. Schwartz*

I've spoken about abundance vs. scarcity and the capacity myth. These are largely issues of mindset. By now, I'm assuming you understand and agree with the principles philosophically. Otherwise, go take a walk, pick up a good novel or watch something entertaining on television instead. Because you're still reading, however, I'm assuming you want to know the next steps in where the rubber meets the road. In this chapter, I'm going to help you set bigger goals so that everyone around you thrives.

As I've mentioned before, I have consulted orthodontists around the country, helping them to identify the shortfalls in their practice. I've helped them to see what it is that they need to do in order to really be successful. I've also noticed that there is a pattern in their thinking and it's one that is holding them back. It's not thinking big or not thinking big enough. Trust me, I get it. Nobody tells us to think big. We are largely raised to think about the short term, choose goals that we know we can achieve, and live on the safe side of choosing things that are manageable.

When we do that, we not only miss out on challenging ourselves, we also hold ourselves back from achieving so much more. How can we ever achieve something big if we can't even think big or set big goals? It's time for you to leave behind the constraints of thinking smaller, safer, and more manageable. I'm challenging you to bust out of those chains, which have been holding you back and to think bigger – a lot bigger. Only when we think big can we actually achieve really big.

Thinking big and bold is not something most people are comfortable with. Once you have been taught to make smaller, easier to achieve goals, you tend to get comfortable there. And then you stay there. Because staying there is, as I mentioned, comfortable and it doesn't make you have to go out of your comfort zone or have to challenge yourself to find ways to meet bigger goals.

If you always stay with the smaller thinking when it comes to your practice, you will always have a smaller practice. It's as simple as that. If nobody has ever said this to you, then you likely never thought about it. Only those who think big will end up going on to achieve big. So, you must ask yourself if you want to achieve small or big. I have a hunch that because you are reading this book, you really do want to achieve big; you are just not sure how to best go about doing that. Hopefully my own experience in thinking big and what it has done for my practice will inspire you and give you the push you need to take your practice to the next level.

Setting Expectations

When I started treating Smiles Change Lives patients, I did what every other orthodontist did. I took one or two patients per year and gave myself a nice "pat on the back" for being a good person. In the grand scheme of my higher sense of purpose, however, this was like spitting in the ocean and expecting it to change the temperature of the water.

I'll never forget when I used to help with the donation telephone calls each year for the cleft palate children we treat each year at no cost. The recession of 2008-2009 was in full swing, and we all falsely assumed our big donors wouldn't want to donate as much as they had last year, because we assumed everyone had taken a huge hit in the stock market.

Because we lowered our expectations, many donors did donate at a lower level, but one donor who was always good for at least $50,000 or $100,000 per year failed to donate at all. We had lowered the top bracket from $100,000 to only $10,000. And what a mistake that was.

After getting this gentleman on the phone, I asked why he didn't donate anything at all that year. He said, "Because I don't think $10,000 will make a difference." I asked if he wanted to donate $100,000 and he said yes.

This was a powerful lesson. I committed to myself and my employees that if we were going to take the time to do something, we were only going to do things that made a difference. Treating one or two kids each year for Smiles Change Lives didn't really make a difference. They had a waiting list of several hundred kids in the Kansas City area, so we decided to take them all.

During October's National Orthodontic Health Month, our offices match a commitment to treat one Smiles Change Lives patient for each new patient starting treatment. We make it a point to tell our patients, parents and referring colleagues of this commitment and the first year we tested this internal marketing strategy, we started 271 patients. When I called Smiles Change Lives and asked how many patients were on their waiting list, they told me there were only 80 or so kids on the list, so we were able to take them all immediately. Over the next year or so, we finished all of those kids and have continued to start more and more, using our October National Orthodontic Health Month promotion as a way to remind cash-paying patients and parents that when they spend their money with our offices, they're spending it with a company that not only does well but also does good in the community.

Here's the secret: I didn't know how we were going to deal with the logistics of treating 271 kids for free in one year, but my team members and I knew we wanted to do something big, so we committed first and figured it out later. Looking back, I should have done it years ago.

Our expectations make a world of difference. Think about the idea of expectations for a few minutes. Our expectations are what we expect to happen. Whether we set them high or low, they are almost always going to meet you there. The expectations you set for your children will usually be met whether they are high or low. The expectations you set for your staff are also going to be met, no matter how high or low they may be. And the expectations you set for the success of your practice are most certainly going to be met.

Take a moment to think about the expectations you have set for the success of your practice. Have you even set any expectations? Or are you just cruising along, taking what happens to come your way? If you have set expectations for the success of your practice, what do they look like and are they big enough? If you are like most orthodontists I've worked with, your expectations are not set nearly as high as they should be. They are comfortable, safe, and manageable. You don't dare put yourself out there, right?

Why is it that we are so afraid to put ourselves out there and really think big? Think about why it is that you back away from making bold claims about what you will accomplish and how highly successful your practice is going to be. There are a variety of reasons why people shy away from thinking big. For starters, as I mentioned, they have been taught from a young age to stick with what is safe and manageable. They have been taught to stick with what they already know they can accomplish so that there's no real challenge there.

Another reason that people don't think big is because they fear failure. They fear that if they fail, they will look foolish, people will laugh at them, or they will be disappointed in themselves. But again, how can we ever achieve big if we are too afraid to think big? Maybe you will fail. So what? What is the worst thing that would happen if you thought big and it didn't happen? Well, you would likely have still gone a heck of a lot farther than you would have thought without thinking big, you probably learned something from the experience, and you will probably feel more comfortable thinking big again the future. That's because you see that nothing terrible happens from not reaching those big goals. But nothing big can happen if you don't have those big goals set.

If you believe you can achieve something, you will achieve it. We rise, or fall, to the expectations that we set for ourselves. The same goes for our staff and our practice as a whole.

I challenge you to think really big, because I know you can meet those goals, and in doing so, you will become a huge success. Believing that you will have great results is going to be the driving force behind achieving them. It all starts with what you think and with the expectations that you put forth.

Think big. Set your expectations high. Believe you can achieve them. Then start working toward them. The way for it to all come to fruition will open up, and you will achieve those results.

Three Lessons

When I decided to think big with taking on Smiles Change Lives patients, there are many things I learned along the way. There are three main lessons that stick with me that are important and valuable. They are lessons that may help you to think and achieve big too.

First, we asked for forgiveness and not permission by tying our commitment to a goal to start more fee-for-service patients. During National Orthodontic Health Month, I promoted, and my market responded with an offer to start one Smiles Change Lives patient for every new start in the practice. It was like Toms shoes. Parents who were going to spend their money on orthodontic treatment somewhere immediately resonated with what we were doing. Affluent people want to spend their money with businesses that make a difference.

So, the first lesson in helping you think bigger in your goals and in chasing down big results are to commit first and figure out the rest later. Stop waiting for the perfect time to do something big. Chances are, it will never be the perfect time. You can always adjust course or change your mind, but sitting on the sidelines is not the way to achieve something big.

There will never be a perfect time to do anything. Waiting for the perfect time to set or move forward with goals is one of the biggest mistakes that people make. Far too often, people have an amazing idea, and it's one that can be life changing for them. So, they keep the idea in their mind, and they keep waiting for all conditions to be right. They say they will get it started when this happens, that happens, or the other. Meanwhile, the energy and drive of their big goal continues to diminish.

When people let their big ideas sit, they tend to go nowhere. While they wait for the perfect time and the perfect conditions, the big idea continues to shrink. After enough time has passed, it is a mere memory. The big idea went flat and nothing came of it. Think about how many times in your life you have had an amazing idea, and you said you were going to do it when the time was right. Well, was the time ever right? If you are like most people, no, the perfect time never arrived, and the idea died.

Don't let your big ideas die. Immediately jump in, and put them into action. That's the only way they are going to go anywhere. Get started,

AS LONG AS YOU THINK SMALL WHEN IT COMES TO YOUR PRACTICE, YOU WILL ALWAYS HAVE A SMALLER PRACTICE. IT'S AS SIMPLE AS THAT.

take the first steps, make the commitment, and let the rest of it all fall into place. And it will fall into place. The only thing keeping you from reaching those big goals is your commitment to getting started. If you don't immediately get started with your big goals, then you will immediately start coming up with excuses that will keep you from ever getting started.

Take the first step, and you will navigate your way along the path toward success.

Second, don't be afraid to make a big, bold claim like starting one Smiles Change Lives patient for every new patient you start next month or next quarter. No one is going to show up at your office and christen you as the most philanthropic orthodontist in your town. That's a position you must self-designate. Claim it for yourself; and then sit back and watch how much publicity and positive press you'll receive.

Yes, it's bold to say that you are going to take on a Smiles Change Lives patient for every new patient your office gets. But that's what thinking big is all about. It's about being bold, stepping out of your comfort zone, and taking on challenges that may scare you a little bit. When we make bold claims, we are setting the expectations for our future. If you want a practice that is a huge success, then bold statements and goals are exactly what you need.

Many people feel that there is something wrong with turning the spotlight on themselves or on their practice. They feel that it is somehow selfish or better left to other people. That's simply not true. There is absolutely nothing wrong with making bold statements about what your office is going to do and then reaping the media rewards as a result. When you help Smiles Change Lives patients, you are doing a good deed. You are helping to change a life for the better and supporting your community in a big way. Your office should be acknowledged for that, and you should in turn have good energy flow your way.

Everything we do in life is like planting seeds. The things we say, the things we do, it's all planting seeds everywhere we go. The seeds you plant are either going to end up growing weeds or beautiful flowers. Which one grows all depends on the type of seeds you are planting along the way. If you plant seeds of negativity, that's what will grow. When you plant seeds of goodness, that is also what will grow. Every time my office helps a Smiles Change Lives patient, we are planting seeds of goodness, compassion, and caring for our community. As those seeds flourish, we get goodness back to us and our office in the way of the community caring for us and showering us with goodness. We get back what it is that we put out.

When an orthodontic practice decides to go big and be bold they are changing lives and making the community a better place, and they are going to reap rewards in return. The media loves it, the parents in the community love it, everyone loves it. What is not to love about a practice doing something like that? That's the type of practice you want your family and friends to know about. That's the kind of story you want your readers to know about.

Third, if you're going to go in, go all the way in. Assign teammates to help you achieve your goals. Circle dates on the calendar. The best invention in the world is the deadline. If you say you're going to treat 50 Smiles Change Lives patients by July 1st, then circle that date on the calendar and make sure you're making progress each month towards that goal.

It's imperative that when you decide to go big that you take action to move in that direction. You don't have to know every little thing you will do from the start. In fact, you will fine-tune your procedure for it as you go along. You are bound to learn what works, what helps to streamline things, and what slows you down. Once you learn these things, you can use that information to shape your goals and navigate your way toward successfully reaching your goal.

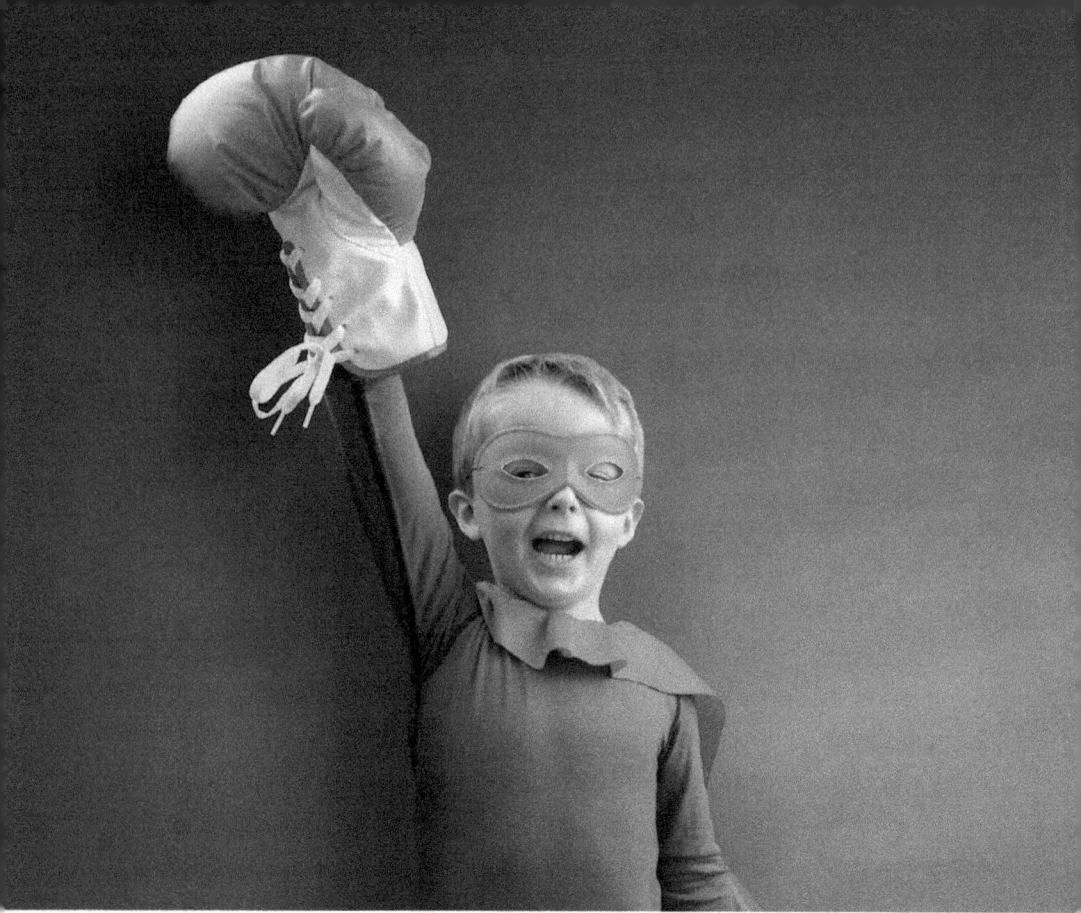

Make the decision and decide what you will do first. You don't have to decide what you will do every step of the way. But get started in the right direction. Give yourself some deadlines; start with what you know you can do. Get your team on board and let them get started with doing what they know they can do. When you come together as a team in order to reach a common goal, you will all be chipping in and helping to achieve it. Collective minds can move mountains and create amazingly successful practices.

Whether you oversee analyzing to ensure progress is being made toward reaching the goals or put a highly motivated team member in charge of it, make sure that someone is keeping track. It's important to monitor the progress to ensure that things are being done every month that are moving you in the right direction. The person who oversees this needs to be someone who is committed to the success of it, knows how to keep people motivated, understands the importance of thinking big, and why achieving this massive goal matters.

Finally, celebrate your wins. The smartest firms and organizations on the planet are extremely generous in sharing credit and celebrating the little wins along the way. If you don't send a monthly employee newsletter to everyone on your team, now is the time to start. Show off your Smiles Change Lives commitment, and remind everyone why they come to work at your office in the first place.

Every Smiles Change Lives patient you help is a huge win. I hope you understand just how important the work you are doing with these patients truly is. It's life-changing work, for them, for you and for your staff. It's also life-changing work for your community. The ripple effect from the work you do with every Smiles Change Lives patient is going to go on to have beneficial output that you won't even see. When you accept a patient who would otherwise not be able to get treatment, you will be changing a life. The life that is changed is going to go on to give back to society in a constructive way. You can't even put a real measure on the far-reaching benefits that come as a result of the work you do with every patient.

With the work you do for these patients being so incredibly important to society, it is only natural that people should know about it. You want everyone in your office to see the faces on the children when they smile and know the numbers of patients that they are helping. It's going to do wonders for their own sense of worth, in that they are contributing to such a wonderful movement.

Make sure that everyone in the office knows about every little success along the way. Whether you send out an employee newsletter, post updates in the front office, share the information on social media, or you do it all to get the word out, just keep making sure that everyone knows about these amazing seeds your office is planting.

Big Thinking Leads to Big Successes

We need only to look around any city to see some examples of entrepreneurs who have thought big and have become highly successful as a result. Take Howard Schultz, for example. A man who grew up in the projects and was poor thought bigger than anyone ever believed would have been possible when it came to coffee houses. When Howard met the owners of Starbucks, then a small Seattle-based coffee house, they had only three locations. Shortly after that, he convinced them to hire him as their marketing and retail director. When they didn't want to take Starbucks in the direction he had envisioned, he walked away and started another coffee company.

Two years later, he went back and purchased Starbucks for $3.5 million. At the time, the chain had six locations and no vision to ever take over the world. But Howard thought differently; he thought big, and his plans in buying it were to make it a household name. While people may have thought his vision was too big or the concept would never work, he proved everyone wrong. Dead wrong.

In his quest to think big, and to think bigger than any competitors, he has grown the chain to having 28,000 stores around the world. The company is not only a household name, but they offer a product that many people feel a connection to and can't seem to do without. In fact, their annual sales top $22 billion worldwide.

And he hasn't stopped there. He continues to think big. He provides every employee full healthcare (even his part-time employees), he pays for employees to earn a college education, and he has a mission to hire 10,000 veterans and their spouses.

Few entrepreneurs think that big. But few entrepreneurs end up reaching that level of success. Today, Howard is personally worth over $3 billion, and Starbucks continues to thrive in business and delight fancy drink

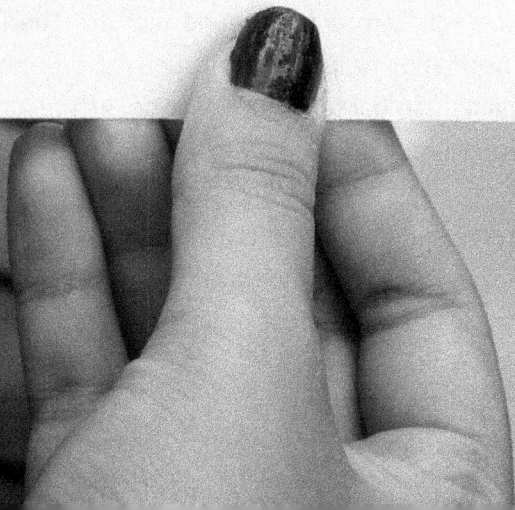

connoisseurs around the world. What would have happened if he would have never had the courage to think big? We may not all be lined up at Starbucks getting our lattes. Big thinking produces big results.

Another entrepreneur who didn't shy away from thinking big was the late, great Herb Kelleher of Southwest Airlines. When he thought big on what the airline's company model should look like, it had three planes. It was a small airline that, because of his vision, grew to be the largest domestic airline service in the country. Unheard of at the time, his big idea was to make airline travel affordable. That vision, which most people likely laughed at, ended up revolutionizing the industry.

Not only did the airline grow to now service around 100 destinations around the country, but it has experienced over 45 years of profitability. When he passed away at the age of 87 in 2019, he was worth an estimated $2.5 billion. Thinking big made him a huge success.

Imagine being born without one of your hands, and then having a dream of being a professional baseball player. That's thinking big, right?

Well, that's exactly what Jim Abbott did. Being born without a hand didn't keep him from thinking so big that he wanted to grow up to be a professional baseball player, a pitcher of all things. Never once did he back down from those big goals, and he went on to reach them.

Not only was Jim a first-round pick for the California Angels in the 1988 draft, but he pitched through 11 seasons in the major leagues. He finished his career with 87 wins, including a no-hitter against the Cleveland Indians.

That's an example of what thinking big can do for someone, despite what others may consider major hurdles. Not thinking big could have deprived us of some of the greatest people ever known.

"Dear Staff & Board,

Thank you so much for this opportunity. You made a very broken hearted girl believe in humanity again. I didn't realize how much it affected me that I could not provide this opportunity for my daughter. My parents were never able to do it for me, and I was just waiting for the word "no" to come out of the provider's mouth. After living a life of "no's" and shut doors, you're always preparing for the bad news. What was even more heartbreaking was seeing that very same look in my daughter's eyes while sitting in the orthodontist's chair. She was prepared for a "no". After working so hard my whole life to pull my children out of poverty, and to not have the same mindset as me, I was saddened to see that it was still passed down. When Dr Miller said, "welcome," it took my breath away. I cried so hard and realized then that this is something that affected me deeper than I realized. Thank you so much. You will never know how grateful we are!"

– Kristel P.

Go Big or Go Home

In "The Magic of Thinking Big," the author says, "Those who believe they can move mountains, do. Those who believe they can't, cannot. Belief triggers the power to do." As I explained, it all starts with what you think you can or cannot do. If you think big, then you can do big, even if you haven't taken
the approach before. You can trigger the power to achieve and move mountains. It's just a matter of believing in yourself enough to want to do it.
We think big by changing the way we have been taught to set goals and go after our dreams. We become mindful of our thoughts and words. We replace doubt with belief in what we are doing. We replace negative talk with positive talk. And we set goals and timelines and then work like hell to achieve them. To be someone who thinks big, you must start talking big and using the vocabulary to help you see it through.

Begin to pay attention to your thoughts and words regarding your goals. It's important to use positive words and phrases. Have a vision of what you want to accomplish with your goal and what it will be like when you do. Share that vision in a positive way with others. You and only you determine your value and the value of your practice.

When you go big with the Smiles Change Lives program, you will be agreeing to not sell yourself short. You will be adding value to your office and your staff, and you will be focusing on the objectives.

Now is the time to think big. If you don't, there is a good chance that your competitor is considering doing it right now and may beat you to it. The last thing you want is to see your competitor go big using an idea that you were thinking about doing. Your practice will grow big when you think big. Smiles Change Lives is an effective way to take your practice to the next level. It worked for me, and it can work for you too.

It's time to think BIG.

"My journey...

with Dr. Wazio and Smiles Change Lives is one I will never forget. When my family first discovered Smiles Change Lives, I was about to turn the cut off age for the application eligibility. The situation turned into a race against time. My family scrambled to achieve all the appropriate requisites and allow enough time for them to be processed before my birthday. By the time we had completed everything, we were unsure of the likelihood of my application being approved. I prepared myself for the worst-case scenario and struggled with the idea that I may have crooked teeth for the rest of my life but there is a saying "it is always darkest just before the dawn."

I received a follow up letter not long after, opened it up and read the words "TREATMENT APPROVED". It was the happiest day of my life. Or so I thought...

Fast forward three and a half years, a few broken brackets, and too many lost rubber bands to count to the day I thought would never come.

When I finally got my braces off, I was in a state of disbelief. I looked at a brand-new man in the mirror and couldn't wait to meet him. I was no longer trapped by my self-conscious feelings.

A simple thank you does not begin to express the gratitude I have for Dr. Wazio and his amazing staff. The level of professionalism, kindness, and empathy is unmatched. I have been given a tool that I will treasure for the rest of my life. My newfound confidence and smile have been so empowering. I truly cannot wait for what the future holds for me now. Thank you Dr. Wazio and SCL for changing my life!"

– Nathan W.

CHAPTER 10

MAGNETIC OPPORTUNITY

....

"It is literally true that you can succeed best and quickest by helping others to succeed." – Napoleon Hill

....

Thinking BIG and making exciting commitments to serve your community through Smiles Change Lives is a magnetic opportunity for you. I hope that this far into the book, you are beginning to realize that and see the larger picture in how it will help your office to succeed. Magnetic opportunities are important for any business that wants to do more, go farther, and become more successful.

The mindset and engagement required to step up in a big way will start to magnetically bring new people, opportunities and results into your life. Edward Kramer said, "The hole you give through is the hole you receive through." Think about that for a moment. What is the hole you give through like? If you can't answer that question, or you can identify that, well, it's entirely too small, then you can see why it is that you are getting what you have.

Now is the time to bore a bigger hole in which to give and ultimately in which to receive. The more you send out to the community, the more you are going to get back. There's no better time than the present to start expanding your reach and seeing where it lands you and what it brings you. What would you have to lose by giving more and helping more people? Let's hypothetically say that you decided to go full steam ahead with the Smiles Change Lives program. After a few months of you putting in the time and effort, you can't see anything you have gotten in return. What was your loss? Just some time, in all honesty.

But I say that if that were the case, you didn't at all give it your all. Months into it, if you got nothing in return, then you did something wrong, quite frankly. In all honesty, I'd say you would have to try pretty darn hard to get nothing out of participating in the Smiles Change Lives program. It's such a magnetic opportunity that anyone who gives it half a chance and even puts in half the effort is going to reap rewards.

As I always like to say, you either find a way, or you find an excuse. I've heard every excuse in the book for why someone's office isn't bringing in a slew of new patients each year. You couldn't give me an excuse that I haven't already heard. And you know what? I don't believe any of them. I believe that you will either find a way or you will find an excuse for why you aren't taking the initiative to find a way.

So many doctors fail to open themselves up to exciting opportunities, new and talented employees and bigger results because they see the world through too small a hole. In effect, they've become repellents. By saying no to most new challenges and opportunities like Smiles Change Lives, they never even know all the people and growth that could have been magnetically attracted to their office.

In this chapter, I'm going to delve into something that you may not be familiar with. It's an area of marketing that most people are not familiar with, because it tends to go against the mainstream efforts made by most companies. Yet, because of that very fact, it's something that can help make your practice highly successful and absolutely should not be ignored. We're going to explore the marketing ideas of push versus pull, magnetic marketing, and giving people a reason to pay attention.

Push Vs. Pull

Most marketers push their message into the ether, hoping someone will pay attention. They scream and shout from the mountaintop, but no one hears them. The average consumer is bombarded with marketing and advertising. We're awash in a sea of distraction and confusion in the marketplace. The amount of money that some companies spend on advertising is mind- blowing, to say the least.

It's estimated that marketers will spend around $113 billion in global marketing in 2020. A rule of thumb that many businesses use is to spend at least 1 percent of their sales per year in advertising or marketing. Therefore, if your business were to have $1 million in sales, you would be spending $10,000 per year on advertising. Whether or not you are really getting a great return on those dollars spent is a whole different question. In fact, many people throw the money into marketing and have no idea if they are getting a good return on their investment. If you are not tracking your dollars spent to see what you are getting in return, then you are likely wasting your money.

The point of advertising or marketing is to push people to your practice. The whole idea behind it is to get your name or message in front of the potential buyer, or patient in your case, and have a good enough message that it pushes them to choose your office. The problem with this is that you are probably spending a lot of money to push people to your office. The bigger problem with doing that is that you likely don't need to do that. Not if you take a different approach to bringing in new patients to your office.

Aligning with something like Smiles Change Lives reverses the equation. It draws people to you. They want to know how in the world you can do so much, give so much and be so successful while supporting your community in a way no one else is doing. What you gain from working with Smiles Change Lives is the pull factor. You will take care of patients, but in doing so, you will be pulling people into your office. And you won't be spending thousands of dollars to make it happen. People are going to do it for you through word-of-mouth advertising which is free and the best type of marketing on the planet.

The difference between push and pull marketing all comes down to how you are approaching your potential customers. When you spend money on advertising, you are pushing people to you, which takes a lot of effort and money. When you focus on pull marketing, you are building your brand, and you are creating a patient base that is loyal and will want to do business with you. They will be so loyal and believe in what you are doing to the point that they will help pull others to your practice as well.

Obtaining a new patient through advertising is nice, but it doesn't have anything to do with loyalty. When loyalty is involved, you will have customers that are there for the long haul, who believe in your office. They will want to help you succeed, so they will be your grassroots-level marketing team that helps to spread the good name of your office.

Businesses that focus on push marketing tend to spend their efforts taking their product or service to the people. They will chase them down trying to show what they can do and sell them on their services.

On the opposite end of the spectrum, pull marketing focuses on bringing the patients to you. Word-of-mouth advertising, or referrals, is one of the most effective ways to engage in pull advertising. You are essentially pulling people into your office through the good word on the street. They hear good things, they respect your office, and they want to do business with you. When people hear good things are happening somewhere, they are drawn to it and want to be a part of it. They want to support what is happening.

It's a different concept for most people to grasp at first, because it's so new to them. We have forever been bombarded with paid advertising messages, so it makes it seem as though that's the norm and that's the best thing for businesses to do. But I'm here to tell you, it's not.

When you engage in push marketing efforts, you will always be looking for your next patient. On the other hand, when you engage in pull marketing, your next patient is always presenting themselves, ready for you.

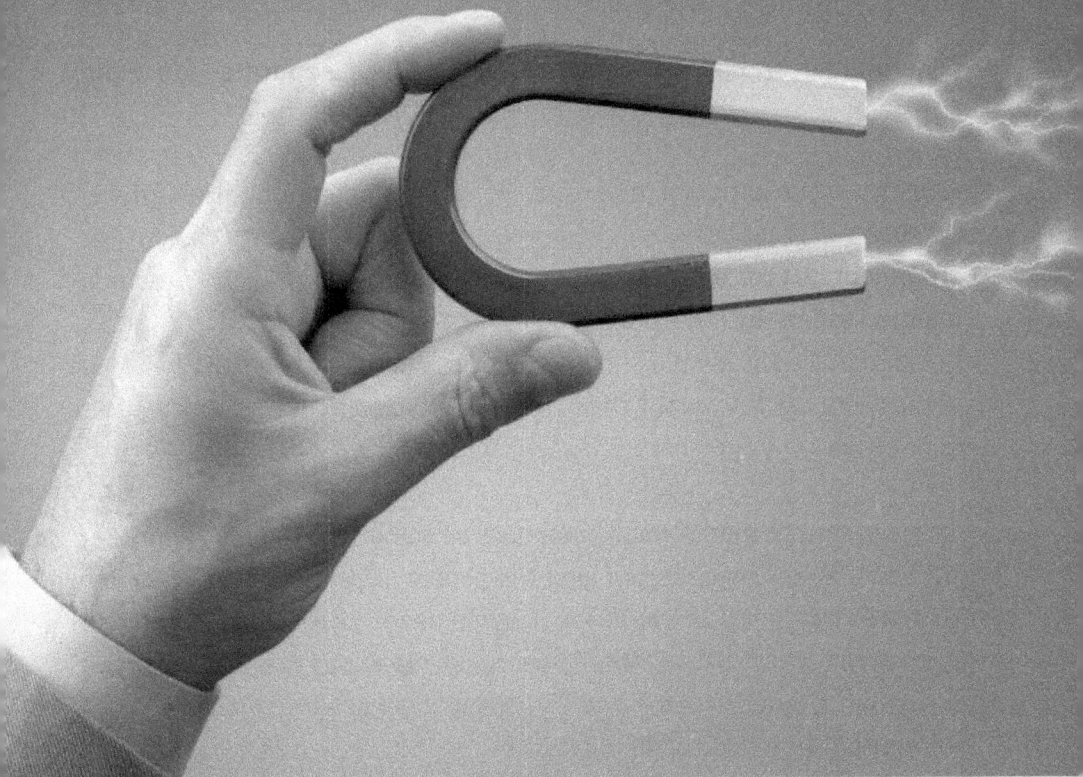

Magnetic Marketing

Magnetic marketing, a phrase and concept created by my friend and marketing mentor, Dan Kennedy, who created and worked on some of the world's top brands like Proactive, Miracle Ear and Weight Watchers, is all about answering the question, "Given all my options in the marketplace, including the option of doing nothing, why should I, as a prospective new patient of yours, pay attention to you?"

Think about how many choices consumers are bombarded with daily. Heck, if you go to the deodorant aisle in the store, it can be a daunting task to make a choice. There are rows, five shelves high, with various kinds of deodorants. Different brands, scents, sizes, you name it. Consumers tend to have a ridiculous amount of choices when it comes to just about anything they purchase.

Differentiate or die. Let Smiles Change Lives separate you from the pack.

Consider your practice and that of your competitors. How many orthodontic practices are in your area, or how many other choices for treatment do your potential patients have? Most people have numerous choices, especially if they live in a decent-sized city. So, what is it that is going to make the people choose you over your competitors? What will make them say they want their treatment or their child's treatment at your office?

That's magnetic marketing. There must be something that you are doing that acts as the magnet, bringing the people to you. It's the "it" factor that will be the deciding reason why someone chooses your practice over all the others. If you haven't yet taken measures to ensure that you have that magnetic factor, and I'm assuming you haven't, then you are missing out on a huge opportunity.

Something must set your office apart. Your potential patients need a reason to call your office for an appointment. Otherwise, all things are considered equal, and they may as well throw a dart at the wall or close their eyes and see where their finger lands. That's not the most effective way to choose where to get treatment, as you can imagine. Such tactics tell you literally nothing about the doctor's integrity, reputation, outlook, philanthropy, etc.

These are issues that patients care about more than you may realize, and they will be the reason that they are drawn to one office over another.

If you are not doing something to engage in magnetic marketing and your competitor is, guess what? Your competitor is going to leave you in the dust when it comes to the volume of new patients they will be seeing.

WHEN PEOPLE HEAR A STORY
ABOUT SOMEONE DOING GOOD AND
MAKING A BIG DIFFERENCE IN THE
COMMUNITY, THEY CAN'T HELP BUT
TO TELL SOMEONE ELSE ABOUT IT.

You don't want to let that happen, and it is well within your power to not let it. Magnetic marketing is going to draw people to you, just like a magnet. Working with the Smiles Change Lives program is an effective magnetic marketing tool that ends up bringing a steady stream of new patients to your office.

When you treat Smiles Change Lives patients, you are branding your image and creating a reputation. It's one that will draw people to you like a magnet. People in the community will know the good work you do to help change lives, one smile at a time, and they will want to support your efforts. They will want to be associated with your office.

Line up all the orthodontic offices in your area and then have one of them be an office that provides free treatment to kids who need it and can't afford it. That one office supports the community in a big way. That one office helps to change the lives of kids so that they can grow up having the confidence they need to get more out of life and go on to be a well-adjusted adult. Now, I ask you, which office would you choose to take your child to for treatment or refer your family and friends for treatment? You would choose the one with the magnetic attribute, which is the one that works with Smiles Change Lives, without a doubt.

Smiles Change Lives is magnetic marketing for any orthodontist office that takes it on and is all in. It's just that simple, just that effective.

Turning Heads

In 2015, I was named The Kindest Kansas Citian, and I believe it had everything to do with my affiliation with Smiles Change Lives. People saw the work that I was doing to help the community, especially to help change the lives of children, and they wanted to acknowledge me for my generosity. They can't bestow the award on me every year, even though I'm still doing the same kind work today, but the reputation has already been established.

When people realize that you are doing something that is kind, they want others to know. Why is that, you ask? Look around you. Our world is bombarded with negativity. The constant flow of news stories that we hear remind us that there is a lot of negativity out there. The stories and headlines are filled with those who take from society, harm society, and do little in the way to help make a difference.

When a story comes around that is the opposite of that, people sit up and take notice. People are craving stories that remind them that their fellow humans deep down are truly good and giving beings. They truly do. It gives them a boost and makes them feel good. It restores their faith in humanity when they hear about people doing things that are selfless. These are the stories the press craves, and they are the stories that the people love.

When people hear a story about someone doing good and making a big difference in the community, they can't help but to tell someone else about it. The next thing you know, a dozen people have heard what is going on. As each person begins to tell someone else, the ripple effect grows bigger and bigger. Within that, you and your story are reaching more people than you ever thought you could. But you are doing so in a way that you didn't pay for. Instead, you used pull marketing, you used magnetic marketing, and you gave people a reason to choose you over your competitors.

You absolutely must give people a reason to choose you over your competitors. Up until this point, you probably haven't done that or you haven't done something in a way that really stands out. The Smiles Change Lives program does exactly that. It gives your potential patients a huge reason to choose your office over competitors, and it makes your office stand out. People will feel good knowing that they are helping your office make it possible to change the lives of young people, one smile at a time.

I've mentioned before, and it's an important point worth bringing up again: The last thing you want to be in your field is boring. Nobody pays attention to boring. The boring office is going to just make it and never reach its full potential. The boring orthodontist will always take the safe route and never be challenged to be amazing. Boring is something that nobody cares about — not the people in your community, not your patients, and not even your competitors. Heck, if you are boring, your competitors are not even looking your way. Why? They already know you are not doing a damn thing to make someone choose your office over theirs. They already have your number and don't need to waste time keeping up on what you are doing anymore.

Be anything but boring. Boring shouts, "don't look at my office; I have no reason for you to look over here." And that's exactly what will happen. Nobody will look your way. You need to stand out, be bold, and go big.

When you work with the Smiles Change Lives program, you are doing just that. Boring people don't go on a mission to give a couple of hundred kids per year free orthodontic treatment. Who takes on such a mission? Those who are leaders, shakers, and trailblazers. That kind of person is anything but boring, and those are the kind of people who get noticed. They get noticed in a big way, by everyone from their current patients to potential patients to the media, because changing the world, my friends, is anything but boring.

When you give people a reason to pay attention to what you are doing, they will. They will ask questions, share your stories, refer their friends and family members, and they will respect what your team does. They will see the difference you and your staff are making in the community, and they are going to love it. People need a reason to pay attention; it's your job to give them one. Smiles Change Lives has made it simple for you to give them that reason.

Going Forward

As I said in the beginning of this chapter, Smiles Change Lives is a magnetic opportunity. I don't say this as someone trying to get you do something I have no experience with. On the contrary, I am such an advocate of this program because I have seen and felt the amazing effects it has had on my practice. I have seen what taking on the patients has done for my staff and our reputation, to help people in the community and to bring in a wealth and steady flow of new patients.

I can't say enough good things about Smiles Change Lives.
I can tell you first and foremost that there is one life that I absolutely know that it has changed. Mine.

The program has been a life-changer for me because of all it has done as a result of me choosing to get involved with it. I'm so confident about the merits of this program that I believe wholeheartedly that it will do the same for your office. That's why I put myself out there, sharing my secrets about what it has done for my practice. Most people who have gained so much from being involved in something like this would want to keep it a secret, so that they don't have others competing and gaining from it. Well, I'm different. I want you to succeed. I want every orthodontist in the country to be highly successful. That's why I share my knowledge and experience with Smiles Change Lives and tell you how impactful it can be for your practice.

Smiles Change Lives, and by taking on these patients, you will find that the most profound change happens to you.

CHAPTER 11

PUT IT ON AUTOPILOT

"I think that's the single best piece of advice: constantly think about how you could be doing things better and questioning yourself." – Elon Musk

There's an old saying in direct-response marketing, something I've become somewhat famous for teaching and implementing for doctors all over the globe, and it references a campaign or strategy that achieved excellent results but has now fallen off our radar. We say, "we stopped doing it because it worked." It's a tongue-in-cheek reference to the tendency in human nature to only pay attention to the squeaky wheels in our businesses and in our marketing.

We don't give enough attention to the things that work. We take them for granted and forget about them because they worked. We don't give enough attention to our best employees. Instead, we focus on the mediocre or under-performing employees, desperately trying to get them to perform at average levels. That's like the basketball coach ignoring the starting five and only spending her time with the bench. It makes no sense, but we do it all the time in business.

Dropping the Ball

As I mentioned, when things are working in our practice or in any business, we tend to cruise along, not paying much attention to them. It's our shortcomings that tend to get most of our attention. But cruising through the months and years like that can lead to disaster. This is because you are failing to put your finger on what is working, acknowledging it, and holding on tight.

One business that stands out as a shining of example of this happening is Cadillac. For 60 years, Cadillac was the undisputed leader when it came to luxury cars and all it stood for. For decade after decade, it continued, not paying attention to what it was that was working. So essentially, it stopped doing what worked, and when that happened, it was disastrous for the company.

In 1998, for the first time in 60 years, Lincoln surpassed Cadillac in luxury car sales. This was big news because Cadillac was cruising along and then it started making some changes that led to its downfall. In the 1990s, it came out with the Escalade, which is credited with saving the company. Still, it's left the luxury car company with an image problem. In 2017, it was ranked 27th out of 31 brands on vehicle dependability.

A company that was once referred to as "The Standard of the World" has been left trying to figure out how to get back to where it once was. What was it that worked for it and catapulted it to the top of its division? Cadillac had taken it for granted to the point that it doesn't even know and can't put its finger on it. Since the brand has been faltering, it has been trying to figure out what it is that kept it on top for so long. The company is trying a multitude of things to regain its market share. It even moved its headquarters out of Detroit in 2015. Cadillac thought the new swanky Manhattan location would give it a new image and help it get back its high-end status.

It didn't work, and in 2018, the company announced that it would be going back to its roots. It was going to try to get back to what it was that put it on top in the first place including moving its headquarters back to the city of its birth, Detroit, the Motor City.

For those of us on the outside looking in, we have a different perspective. We can see that Cadillac was at its peak for many years, and it took things for granted. When it took things for granted, it ended up losing focus, which eventually led to it seeing a ton of customers make a shift to imports and other luxury brand vehicles. Cadillac is a stark example of why you should never take your position in the marketplace for granted.

Always strive to find new ways to capture the hearts and minds of your customers and to nurture those relationships.

Smiles Change Lives is a critical component to our position in the market. If I failed to put effort and focus into the relationship with Smiles Change Lives, I suspect my fate would be the same as Cadillac in the 1970s and 1980s. One of the reasons that my practice is so successful is because I don't take what works for granted. I see what works, and I continue to keep it well-oiled and humming along. That's the only way that you can have a practice that is a huge success. If you overlook or take for granted that which is working for your practice, then you will experience what Cadillac did. You will be left scratching your head, throwing darts at the wall, and trying to figure out what it was that made you so successful. You'll spend your time and effort trying to find out what worked when you should have been acknowledging it and managing it all along.

Sustaining Practices

Previously in this book, we discussed how your Smiles Change Lives patients can become your full-time marketing department, however, it is also highly effective at sustaining your practice from within. Your affiliation with the program shines a positive light on what you do and helps you attract top talent. It can quite literally change your life, and then a few years into the program, your tendency will be to forget how great it works and to let your attention slip.

Trust me when I say that it's easy to take the program and all that it's doing in your practice for granted. Week after week, you see that your practice is growing and is doing fantastic. You know you are doing something right, but there's a good chance you will fail to point the finger in the right place. The magic with Smiles Change Lives happens behind the scenes. There's a ripple effect that ends up touching many lives and it, in turn, sends you a lot of patients. You will begin getting referrals on a regular basis, but if you are not careful, you will forget why you are now getting all these referrals.

Instead of forgetting what works, make sure you set aside time each quarter and each year to recommit to your goal to treat more Smiles Change Lives patients. Celebrate the wins with your team. Show off the exceptional results for your Smiles Change Lives patients, and put this program on autopilot by incorporating your Smiles Change Lives goals with your practice goals, as well as talking about them at each monthly team meeting, and at your quarterly and annual planning retreats.

By putting the Smiles Change Lives program on autopilot, you will be committing to the idea that it is going to be a long-term, standard part of your practice and business model. Yet, just like any long-term commitment in your life, you can't take it for granted. You must renew your commitment to it, and celebrate the successes that it brings to you.

Think about how many people you know who have an exercise program. Granted, most people don't exercise regularly, but there are some people who have made it a regular ongoing part of their life. Their health is in good condition, they are at a healthy weight, and they keep cruising along. What would happen if they took for granted the benefits they were getting from that daily exercise? Sure, from day to day, they can't see the benefits of making sure they get their daily walk or run in, but in the background, it's doing wonders for their body. If they take it for granted and stop the daily exercising, or reduce their commitment to it, they will surely see that their health benefits begin to diminish from the reduction in their effort.

It's the same with Smiles Change Lives. When you continue renewing your commitment to the program, you will continue reaping the rewards that it brings. If you falter, it's like anything else that you slip up on or give up on; you will lose the benefits. If you take those benefits for granted, there's a good chance you will not realize that it is the source

"LET'S CREATE THE KIND OF WORLD WE WANT TO LIVE IN."

— SIR RICHARD BRANSON

behind the success of your practice, and it will have a detrimental impact. Learn from Cadillac's mistakes. Be mindful of all that being a part of the program is doing for you, so that you renew your commitment to it and continue to experience growth and success within your practice.

Changing the World

I'm a fan of Sir Richard Branson, the founder of Virgin Group. He's someone who has used his skills and ingenuity to climb his way to becoming successful. Highly successful, I might add. In fact, his story is fascinating if you, like me, are intrigued by entrepreneurial success stories. He's a man who is self-made, making his first leap at starting a business over 50 years ago. Today, he has a net worth over $4 billion.

There is a lot that we can learn from this high school dropout about how we can succeed in our own practices. While his business may have a different focus and a much larger reach, the principles for success are much the same. Richard once said, "Let's create the kind of world we want to live in." He also told the world that he believes businesses have the power to make the world a better place. He shares that only when we come together will we be able to solve the big problems of our time.

He then posed a question to entrepreneurs. He asked, "what is your business doing to change the world?"

That's an important question and one that is well worth pondering. I've said for many years that it's important that orthodontists remember exactly what it is that they are selling. They don't sell treatment services or braces. Not at all. What we sell is a better, more confident lifestyle. Our end product is someone who loves what they see when they look in the mirror, and who feels comfortable applying for jobs, asking people out on dates and smiling in front of people. We make people feel good about themselves.

That's what we have to offer the world – a better feeling, a happier, more content life.

But you take it a step further when you work with Smiles Change Lives. That's one way we are changing the world. Is there something more you can do? If so, why are you not doing it? If not now, then when? There's no better time than the present to start changing the world for the better and creating the type of society we all want to live in. Smiles Change Lives is an effective tool that helps you do that.

Autopilot Your Way Toward Success

When I say, "to put things on autopilot," it's important to have an idea of what I'm referring to. Oftentimes, people think that when something is on autopilot that it's not being looked at, or it's not getting much attention. They believe that things that are boring or mundane are put on autopilot.

Some may feel that mind-numbing tasks are those that are put on autopilot, because you don't need to think about them to get them done. I'm not referring to these negative ideas that are out there regarding putting something on autopilot. I'm using the idea in the complete opposite terms, and want you to do the same.

What I'm referring to by putting your practice on autopilot is that I want you to create the course for success and then continue doing the things that help you reach the level of success you'd like and to grow your practice. Then you let the universe do what it does, and let the magic happen. You continue moving along on that course, no matter what happens, so that you reach your goals.

When you put your practice on autopilot, you are committing to a course for your success.

Committing to a course for success means that you have a plan that you believe will be successful in helping to grow your business and make

your office highly successful. Nothing happens overnight in anything that one does, so you continue to plug along, following the course, and after a while, all those efforts add up to great things. Along the way as you are auto piloting your way toward success, you stop and take a look to see if you are still on the right course. That is the only way that autopilot truly works.

At the heart of your practice being on autopilot is a team that understands the goals and commitment. Only with a team that is on board and understands this will your practice stay the course and be successful at reaching its goals. Their skills and commitment in their daily duties and interactions with people will make a world of difference in your success. Their attitude is going to help make or break your success, so in order for your practice to succeed on autopilot, you have to first ensure that they understand what you are doing, why you are doing it, and the importance of staying committed to it.

The Smiles Change Lives program gives your team a sense of purpose and renews their commitment to your office and its success. They are at the heart of your autopilot vision working. With them, you will succeed. Success isn't something you can achieve all on your own, because your practice, like mine, is multifaceted. You need a great team to ensure that your office is staying the course, holding them accountable, and renewing their commitment.

The Smiles Change Lives program gives your team a sense of purpose and renews their commitment to your office and its success. They are at the heart of your autopilot vision working. With them, you will succeed. Success isn't something you can achieve all on your own, because your practice, like mine, is multifaceted. You need a great team there along with you to ensure that your office is staying the course, following the plan, holding them accountable, and renewing their commitment.

This is where I want to remind you about the importance of empowering your team. Give them the power to help make decisions and keep the program going on autopilot. They want and need to be empowered. Not empowering employees is one of the biggest mistakes that a company can make, and it will always hold you back from success. Learn from those companies that are wildly successful. They always empower their employees.

Walt Disney knew the importance of empowering those on his team. Today, you can walk up to any one of Disney's employees, who are referred to as cast members, and they will go above and beyond to help you. They don't run to a phone or call their boss over to ask how to make things right or help you. They are empowered and will take it upon themselves to do everything they can to make things right and help your family have an amazing time. This is not somewhere that Disney got lucky. It didn't just happen that Disney found people who understand the mission of the company. They were trained and motivated in that they want it to be seen and felt as the Greatest Place on Earth. They get it, and they get it in a big way.

Empowering employees, or cast members, means that everyone is on board with the mission and will go way out of their way to ensure that it succeeds. They will not feel that they are an insignificant and replaceable part in an overall picture. They will feel as though they are part of what is going on.

They will feel engaged, and they will love what you are doing to change the world. Empowering your staff is always a great way to help your relationship with Smiles Change Lives succeed and help your practice succeed.

Your employees need to feel a sense of purpose, and Smiles Change Lives gives them that, especially when you empower them to be a major part of the program. Once you explain what the program is and how it changes lives, they will want to be a big part of that. Let them be and your office will gain in many ways. They will love what they do, they will feel good about what they are contributing to, and the energy that this creates will be unstoppable.

Create the Vision

The job of a great coach isn't to merely tell players on the team what to do and how to do it. The job of a great coach is to create a vision. It's the same thing with your practice and working with Smiles Change Lives. The last thing you want to do is just tell your team you are implementing this program and then lay out a list of what they will be expected to do. Chances are, you won't get great results that way. Be a great coach and create the vision.

Start by creating the vision of how your office will commit to the Smiles Change Lives program. Envision how many people you will help, how your employees will be engaged and what the community will receive as a result of your commitment.

Once you have the vision, share that with your team. A great coach has the winning vision and shares that with the team. They help the team achieve it by identifying strengths in each of their team members and telling them how they can use those strengths to help make the vision a reality. Once you have your team on board with the vision, they will want to help make it a reality.

Ask your team if they want to change the world. Ask them if they want to help kids become more confident, be bullied less, and go on to live happier lives. Then share with them that your office is going to do exactly that by partnering with the Smiles Change Lives program. With the vision there, your team members will each play their part to help make it happen.

CHAPTER 12

LEAVING A LEGACY OF CARING WITH SMILES CHANGE LIVES

"The way to get started is to quit talking and start doing." – Walt Disney

By now, you should have a great idea of what the Smiles Change Lives program is all about. You should also know how your participation can be life changing – not only for the patients you provide treatment to but also for yourself and your team.

I've gone to great lengths in my career to share the secrets to success with my colleagues. I've written numerous books, newsletters and other materials on the subject. I've given countless talks at conferences and mastermind sessions, and I've done many one-on-one coaching sessions with orthodontists. I do this because I truly want every orthodontist to succeed as much as I have, and because I want to elevate the profession.

I'm probably the most outspoken advocate of the Smiles Change Lives program, and the reason is that I firmly believe in its ability to make an enormous difference in the life of a child who is in need of treatment but does not have access due to financial reasons. But this is not a case of me seeing this only as an observer. The program has helped my practice grow exponentially. It has changed the lives of the patients we have treated, my own life, and the lives of my team. It has been nothing short of incredible, and I have no doubt that any orthodontist who makes the commitment to the program and sees it through will become an amazing success.

As an orthodontist, you already know that a smile can change everything for a child. In today's world where young people may feel like they are on display more than ever, maintaining a healthy sense of self-esteem can be an incredibly difficult challenge. Having crooked teeth and a smile they are embarrassed to show only adds to their self-consciousness, and that is an issue that many of these children carry well into adulthood. Making people feel better about themselves is a wonderful way to do your part to make the world a better place. By participating in the SCL program, you are doing more than your "job" of straightening teeth. You are helping children obtain the healthy smile they deserve, and you are creating a legacy for yourself and your practice that you and your team can be extremely proud of.

Reaching Your Goals

I often joke with clients who have hired me to help grow their practices that ultimately, we all have the same exit strategy; in the end, we'll all be equally dead. It lightens the mood for the discussion I really want to have with the client, which is this: nothing you acquire or achieve on this earth is more important than the time that you spend giving love to and helping others.

We have all heard the old expression "you can't take it with you" and when it comes to things like money or possessions, it is true. It's important to recognize that as someone who is in the profession of helping others achieve their "smile goals" - that you should also have some goals of your own. To be successful should be one of them, yes...but to make a real difference in the lives of others using the talents and resources you have been given should without a doubt be another.

I've never seen a U-Haul behind a hearse.

One of the goals that should be included in your road map to success is figuring out what your exit strategy should be. In developing what that should be, you should be asking yourself a few questions. What have I really done with the time I have spent in my practice? What kind of relationships have I developed and nurtured with patients and my team? How much help, love and compassion have I given to others?

WITHOUT A DEADLINE, A GOAL IS REALLY JUST A DREAM.

I have no doubt in my mind that participating in Smiles Change Lives can dramatically improve your answers to these questions. This may be the first time that you have thought about this topic, because, let's face it - it's not one that people really talk about. But ultimately the long-term goal for any orthodontist is to retire from the practice and allow it to not only continue but thrive.

I will tell you that I have thought a lot about this subject, and it brings me great comfort to know that I have a winning exit strategy – because I know that I have put a program in place that has enriched the lives of everyone it has touched. Sure, we may not be able to take anything with us when we go – not even our beloved practices that we put our hearts and souls into for so many years. We can't take with us all the things we purchased either. However, what we can take with us is the satisfaction that we made a difference in this world. That is an accomplishment that you cannot put a value on, because it is priceless!

What are your hopes, goals, and aspirations for your practice and in your career? Have you thought about them? And more importantly – have you given serious consideration to how you can make them happen?

Now is the time to do that because not living up to those things, as it turns out, is one of the biggest regrets that people have at the end of their life.

A research study published in the journal, "Emotion", that was conducted by Cornell University in 2018 looked at this very issue. They set out to find out what it is that people regret the most when they have reached the end of their lives.

In the study, the researchers identified three elements that come together to make a person's sense of self: the "actual", the "ideal", and the "ought." The "actual" are those attributes that the person feels they possess, while the "ideal" self are those attributes that they wish they would possess. These attributes include your goals, aspirations, hopes, and dreams. The "ought" self, the researchers explain, is the person that people feel they should have been based on their duties and obligations.

The study's conclusion was that peoples' greatest regrets in life are the ones that stem from their failure to live up to their ideal selves. They regret not meeting their goals and aspirations.

Chances are that you have regrets - almost everyone does. And certainly, we are all guilty of putting off goals or things that we want to accomplish. We all lead busy lives, and the tendency to schedule things for "when the time is right" or "someday" is a convenient way to focus on what you may feel is "more important" right now.

The problem with this line of thinking is that "someday" is not a box on the calendar. It doesn't exist. It does not have a deadline and without a deadline, a goal is just a dream.

Many people feel that they should wait until they are inspired to get moving on a plan - but the reality is that the greatest inspiration you can ever get to move towards a goal occurs when you get started. Whatever that thing is that you keep telling yourself you want to do "someday" is the very thing that you should start devising a plan to do today.

When you look back on your career, you don't want to look back on it in regret. You want to know that you met your goals and aspirations. You want to be confident that you did everything in your power to make your practice as successful as possible and that you touched many lives in a positive, caring and compassionate manner. Changing the lives of children by giving them the gift of a healthy smile is a wonderful goal to accomplish, and one that you and your team will be able to proudly claim as part of your legacy.

Building Your Exit Strategy

One of the concerns I hear from many orthodontists is the question of what to do with their practice once they are ready to retire. Much like your personal retirement, this is a subject that requires a great deal of planning. After all, you have invested many years of your time in building the practice. Naturally you want to ensure that it goes into hands that will continue what you have built, and of course, ideally it will continue to help sustain you financially for years to come.

Regardless of how far you may be from retirement - how you run your practice now is going to make a direct impact on what happens when it comes time for you to retire.

Put yourself in the shoes of a younger orthodontist who is looking to purchase a practice, and let's consider a couple of scenarios...

In the first scenario: You have an office that got by for a couple of decades and played it safe. It doesn't stand out as being great, but it doesn't have a poor reputation either. It's just there, and it is flavored vanilla. The only reason people may choose that office over a competitor has more to do with things like proximity to their home or which insurance you accept, not because of anything having to do with service or reputation.

In the second scenario: You have a practice that spent a couple of decades supporting the community and being involved in changing lives. You hear people talking about it in the community, and you have read in the newspaper about how the practice is part of the SCL network of providers, and that it has helped to change the lives of many young people. Because of the office's involvement with the group, it has a stellar reputation and has a steady stream of new referrals that come its way.

Which practice do you want to purchase? It's quite honestly a no-brainer.

Of course, you want the one that has the great reputation and is beloved by the community. Honestly, a great reputation is something that money cannot buy, yet it is one of a practice's absolute greatest assets. Not to mention that owning a practice that has hundreds of patients each year who are raving fans of yours is also something you cannot put a price tag on.

Now, consider how participating in the SCL program can help you accomplish all of this and more while adding the additional benefit of allowing you to sell your practice one day for much more than the average.

Our data suggest that what we are doing is working. For our practices and for top coaching clients who have embraced this model, the goodwill in the practice is so strong that our clients earn substantially higher salaries than the average orthodontist, and go on to sell their practices for much more than the average market sale price.

Even if you have many years left before the day you retire and your most pressing problem is which flip flops to wear on your month-long cruise around the Caribbean, the time to get started on this plan and on building your legacy – is now. Then when you do ultimately sell your practice, you can do so for the price you want and with the knowledge that you created something that has truly made a difference in peoples' lives. Plus, the better you do in selling your practice, the better your retirement years will be. Who wouldn't want that?

How Smiles Change Lives Helps You Define Your Vision

When you are creating any kind of plan, it goes without saying that having a vision of each step you want to take from beginning to end is very important. Yet, there are plenty of people who do not do it; they don't have a vision.

They simply hang their sign, open their doors, and hope that patients just miraculously come into the office.

I have said many times before, but it is worth repeating - hope is not a strategy.

You cannot be successful, especially in the long term, by sitting back and leaving things to chance. You must take steps not only to craft your success but to ensure it. It is within your power to create the exact practice that you want, but the trick is that you must know what that exact practice IS first.

Every orthodontic practice should be able to easily define three specific areas of why they exist in the first place, which includes their mission, their values, and their vision. I've worked with enough practices around the world to know that many orthodontists do not take the time to clearly define these three areas and understand what they truly mean. As a result, they end up stifling their own growth or worse, have unhappy patients who will not return, much less refer anyone else.

As an orthodontist, you are in a powerful position to change people's lives for the better. This should be your mission, and it's something you can accomplish by having as many paths for successful treatment as possible for your patients.

Your values should define how your patients will be treated. It is a commitment to making sure that each person who walks through your door has a great experience from start to finish. It is also an effective tool in obtaining and retaining quality team members for your staff, as people who are patient focused and service oriented will naturally want to work for a practice that is too.

Your vision will clearly define where you want your practice to go and what it would like to accomplish; both now and in the future. This is important to make clear, especially to your staff who will work with you to build on this vision.

The Smiles Change Lives program is an excellent way to tell people what your mission and values are or what your vision is. Working with SCL also shows your community that your office is focused on people, not just payments and builds a goodwill amongst the patients you serve that you could not build by merely advertising or giving away free whitening trays.

It's a bonafide commitment to change lives, one smile at a time.

With my own practices, my vision is to have a wildly successful practice that helps as many people as possible and supports the community in big ways. I have big, really big, goals for my practice. It's that really big thinking that has made all the difference. SCL is an important part of what has helped me to reach my goals, grow my practices, and see the vision for my practices become a reality.

When I first started working with SCL, I was a bit skeptical about what it would do for my practice. But I so strongly believed in what the program is doing that I felt I had to commit to it and see where it took us. I shared my vision with my team and inspired them to get on board, which they embraced fully. We moved forward with a resounding commitment toward its success. I've watched its progress carefully, and as I saw the incredible good that it does, and how much it truly benefits everyone involved, I committed to continuing. Today, I am proud to say that I have treated more children through the program than any other doctor in North America.

Taking the Leap

I'm guessing that if you picked up this book, it was because you are ready to grow your practice and set yourself apart from your competition.

Smiles Change Lives is the perfect opportunity to do just that, all while serving an incredibly worthy cause that makes a real difference in the lives
of real people. Not only will you be giving a child an incredible opportunity to improve their self-confidence and their overall health, but you will be giving your team members an opportunity to be a part of something so much bigger than themselves.

A commitment to Smiles Change Lives also means that you are adding enormous value to your practice which will leave a lasting legacy that you can be proud of.

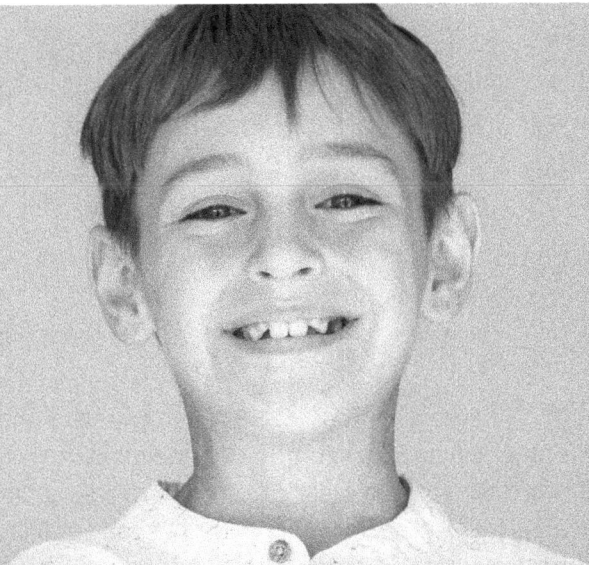

Find out more about getting started by visiting www.SmilesChangeLives.org/for-orthodontists

List of SCL Sponsors and Business Partners

In addition to partnering with orthodontists, Smiles Change Lives has partnered with other businesses to help carry out our mission.

- Dolphin Imaging and Practice Management Solutions
- Jimmy Marketing
- OrthoTown
- Dentma
- Review Wave
- Dentalfone
- Dustin Burleson Seminars
- American Orthodontics
- OrthoArch
- Dentaurum
- Northstar Orthodontics, Inc.
- 3M
- Reliance Orthodontic Products, Inc.
- KR-HR
- Excel Orthodontics
- TruTain
- Easy RX
- Shimmin Consulting
- GrowPracticeGrow
- GOBY

The expression "it takes a village" comes from the African proverb that means it takes an entire community of people who must interact with children for them to experience and grow in a safe and healthy environment. The involvement of these businesses contribute to the win-win-win situation for all parties involved.

This list is ever expanding. If you know of a business that should be included, please reach out to marketing@smileschangelives.org

NOTES

NOTES

NOTES

ABOUT
THE
AUTHORS

ABOUT THE AUTHORS

THOMAS C. BROWN founded Smiles Change Lives with his mother, Virginia Brown in 1997. Smiles Change Lives is an international nonprofit formed under its original name, the Virginia Brown Community Orthodontic Partnership. Virginia grew up during the Great Depression, and her parents could only afford to pay for orthodontic treatment for one of their children.

Virginia's sister was able to get braces while Virginia endured years of teasing and self-consciousness until she finally received treatment during high school. Tom and Virginia, along with Dr. Kelly Toombs, established Smiles Change Lives to help children avoid the physical and emotional difficulties that Virginia herself suffered as a child. Tom has served as Chairman and CEO of Smiles Change Lives since its inception. Tom has been practicing as a business attorney in Kansas City, Missouri for nearly four decades. During this time, he has counseled hundreds of entrepreneurs to organize and grow their businesses, as well as guided numerous non-profits. Additionally, he has owned and operated a number of businesses including restaurants, entertainment businesses and a promotional products company to name a few.

Tom received his bachelors of arts from the University of Pennsylvania and earned his law degree from the University of Michigan. He has written many articles on the subject of business organization and development as well as participated in presenting numerous seminars on this subject.

DR. DUSTIN S. BURLESON is a speaker, teacher, author and orthodontic specialist. Since founding Burleson Orthodontics & Pediatric Dentistry in 2006, thousands of orthodontists have traveled to Kansas City from 28 countries to learn from Burleson's vision to change lives, advance the profession of orthodontics and support his community. Together, he and his students treat hundreds of thousands of patients throughout the world each year.

He writes five professional newsletters monthly, is the director of the Leo H. Rheam Foundation for Cleft & Craniofacial Orthodontics, teaches at both Children's Mercy Hospital and the UMKC School of Dentistry while operating a large multi-clinic orthodontic and pediatric dental practice in Kansas City, Missouri. His practices have personally transformed the smiles of over 22,000 patients right here in Kansas City and he has helped more children through the Smiles Change Lives non-profit organization than any other doctor in North America.

The author of two Amazon best-selling consumer books, "Stop Hiding Your Smile!" and "The Consumer's Guide to Invisalign," Dr. Burleson has been invited to speak throughout the world and has shared the stage with celebrities and athletes who mirror his passion to help more people live healthier, happier lives. He's been featured on FOX, NBC, ABC, CBS, CNBC and The Kansas City Star. A two-time Inc. 500 | 5000 honoree recognized for building one of the fastest-growing orthodontic specialty practices in North America, Dr. Burleson was also awarded the American Dental Association's prestigious Golden Apple Award in 2014 and the Missouri Dental Association's Outstanding Dental Leadership Award in the same year. Dr. Burleson provides over $1 million in free orthodontic care to cleft lip and palate children each year.

His practices have worked with the prestigious Disney Institute and Ritz Carlton to bring the same "wow" experience to the smiles of patients both young and old. Asked what makes his practice different, Burleson quickly replied with a warm smile, "It's our people, our culture, and our commitment to do whatever it takes to serve the best interest of our patients and their families." He continued, "even if that means referring them to a cheaper option in town, or to one of his non-profit foundations, when parents are unable to afford treatment at a Burleson facility." Burleson's offices at last count have over 22,000 satisfied patients, traveling from cities as far away as Chicago, New York and San Francisco to be treated by one of Burleson's certified smile specialists.

www.ingramcontent.com/pod-product-compliance
Lightning Source LLC
Chambersburg PA
CBHW071352280326
41927CB00041B/2943